# *Writing Rules!*

## Other Beeline Books Include:

The Publishing Center
*How to Create a Successful Publishing Center in Your School,
        Church, or Community Group*

The Treasured Mailbox
*How to Use Authentic Correspondence with Children, K–6*

Inside the Classroom
*Teaching Kindergarten and First Grade*

Write-A-Thon
*How to Conduct a Writing Marathon in Your
        Third- to Fifth- Grade Class*

The Magical Classroom
*Exploring Science, Language, and Perception with Children*

Walk This Way!
*Classroom Hikes to Learning*

Kids on the 'Net
*Conducting Internet Research in K–5 Classrooms*

The Young Author Festival Handbook
*What Every Planner Needs to Know*

Look—and Learn!
*Using Picture Books with Children Grades Five and Up*

Hit Enter
*50+ Computer Projects for K–5 Classrooms*

# *Writing Rules!*
## *Teaching Kids to Write for Life, Grades 4–8*

## Mike Brusko

Heinemann
Portsmouth, NH

Heinemann
A division of Reed Elsevier Inc.
361 Hanover Street
Portsmouth, NH 03801–3912
http://www.heinemann.com

*Offices and agents throughout the world*

Library of Congress Cataloging-in-Publication Data
Brusko, Mike.
    Writing rules! : teaching kids to write for life, grades 4–8   /
Mike Brusko.
        p.   cm.
    Includes bibliographical references.
    ISBN 0-325-00157-X
    1. English language—Composition and exercises—Study and teaching
(Elementary)—United States.   I. Title.
LB1576.B876   1999
372.62'3'044—dc21                                                99-26109
                                                                      CIP

Editor: Amy L. Cohn
Production: Elizabeth Valway
Interior design: Greta D. Sibley & Associates
Cover design: Darci Mehall, Aureo Design
Manufacturing: Louise Richardson

Printed in the United States of America on acid-free paper
03 02 01 00 99 ML  1 2 3 4 5

*To*
*my parents, for their guidance;*
*my children, for their innocence;*
*and my wife, for her inspiration and confidence.*

# Contents

 # *Acknowledgments*

I'll always remember the faculty at Friendship Elementary School in Coatesville, PA, and late Principal Joe Hollister, for their encouragement and acceptance during my first professional teaching experience. Likewise, George DeVault, a great writer and my first editor, taught me a lot of what's in this book.

Finally, special thanks to Heinemann project editor Amy L. Cohn, who never stopped believing that this book needed to be published.

# *Writing Rules!*

# *Introduction*
## *Let's Teach Writing as a Life Skill*

My seventeen-year-old daughter loves writing personal letters. And she writes great ones. They're funny, compelling, detailed without being tedious—and inquisitive without being nosy.

But she cringes when she has to write anything with a more formal purpose behind it.

A cover letter to go with a job application? An essay focusing on a single question or issue?

"I hate writing stuff like that," she'll complain. "I can never think of anything cool to say."

If she were the exception, I wouldn't be writing this book. But she's not. In fact, after more than twenty years of teaching people to write in classrooms and in the business world, I've come to believe that writing may be the most hated and misunderstood of all routine human activities.

I got my first inkling of this while teaching fifth grade in the late '70s and early '80s. It became almost an obsession of mine to motivate students to write for fun during spare class time. I even sold an article to a magazine for teachers about some of my techniques.

But the effect was temporary. Before long, kids who'd finished their seatwork went right back to daydreaming, doodling, and visiting the bathroom.

And as you can guess, their writing didn't improve. They still misused big words in an attempt to sound scholarly in social studies essays. And they still managed to write three-page book reports without ever summarizing the main plotline or theme.

Teachers tell me things haven't changed much since then. "I'd love it if my students enjoyed writing more," a teacher friend said recently. "I try never to give the same assignment twice, but I still get groans."

When I left teaching for the business world, I discovered that write-o-phobia isn't just a childhood disease. Most of the adults I've worked with during the past seventeen years—which includes clerical and unskilled labor-ers as well as highly paid professionals—fear writing just as much as kids do.

Like my daughter, they'll do almost anything to avoid putting their ideas or complaints down on paper. "Can't I just leave you a voice mail?" they'll plead. When they finally do force themselves to write something, the final product is usually a convoluted, cliché-ridden mess. I end up call-ing them to find out what they're really trying to say beneath all those words.

I'm convinced that the solution to all this lies in a different approach to teaching writing in middle school and junior high. Specifically, I'd like to see our schools formalize writing instruction and emphasize clarity and effec-tiveness above all else. By "formalize," I mean: teach writing every day.

"I already do that," says one of my teacher friends. "We do DOL every day, and we have whole language. . . ." Granted, whole language and those fix-the-errors blackboard lessons known as Daily Oral Language have greatly increased the amount of writing kids *do* in school nowadays. But they haven't necessarily increased the amount of writing that kids *learn*. (Think of it this way: Just because kids eat lunch in the school cafeteria every day doesn't mean they learn proper table manners.)

The only way to really teach the basics of good writing is with a true writing curriculum: benchmarks, definable goals, step-by-step skill-build-ing, and objective evaluation tools. Excluded from my ideal writing curricu-lum would be many subjects long considered part of traditional writing instruction. Mainly, penmanship, spelling, and rules of grammar. We rou-tinely mistake these for good writing. Actually, they're only the materials of written communication. You can master all of them and still be an ineffec-tive writer.

We need to continue teaching these skills, of course. But I believe we should keep them separate from writing instruction until kids are old enough to incorporate them naturally, without losing their focus on good writing mechanics. When we give a writing assignment, we should do so with a specific writing skill in mind. And we should evaluate kids on how well they demonstrate *only* that skill. If they commit an error in spelling or grammar, we should flag it and correct it. But we shouldn't deduct points for it until kids are well into high school.

It's unrealistic to think middle school and junior high students can give equal attention to effective writing, accurate spelling, and proper grammar, all at the same time. Especially when their main concern is meeting your "at least three-to-five pages" requirement.

And it's flat wrong to assume any of those skills is more important than the others.

We need to teach language mechanics (punctuation, grammar, and spelling) separately from writing when kids are young, and combine them gradually as students improve at each.

I also propose we reduce our emphasis on "voice" and "creativity" when we teach writing. "But, voice is what gives writing its personality," my teacher friends tell me. They're right, of course. But voice and personality are byproducts of good writing, not means for achieving it.

Our focus on voice reflects our mistaken belief that writing is, above all, a form of self-expression. Virtually all writing that people need to do in their jobs and everyday lives is about communication, not self-expression. There's a profound difference between the two. Self-expression puts the focus on me, the writer. Communication puts the focus on you, the reader. Effective writing focuses on the reader first.

Playing up "creativity" adds to kids' confusion about writing. To begin with, it suggests to them that good writing requires a good imagination. A good imagination helps if you're going to be a professional fiction writer who'll earn a living entertaining people with clever stories. But our main goal isn't to train future poets and authors. It's to give kids the writing skills they'll need as adults, no matter what career they choose.

Our emphasis on creativity also encourages wordiness. When students "can't think of anything cool to say," their response is to use more words and bigger words. (What's the most common question kids ask when you give a writing assignment? If it's "How long does it have to be?" then you have first-hand experience with creative writing's most enduring legacy.)

I suggest we teach creative writing as an enrichment activity. Its relationship to everyday classroom writing instruction should be like the relationship between Physical Education class and extracurricular sports. Make it available to students. But don't position it as a skill kids should strive for. Instead, let's emphasize the kind of writing that the world will demand of them: clear, effective, and to-the-point.

A curriculum that would aim us in that direction would focus heavily on these five concepts:

- **Audience and purpose** (visualizing both before you write)
- **Words** (replacing big ones with small ones)
- **Sentences** (maximizing impact while economizing words)
- **Paragraphs** (synthesizing all of the above)
- **Rules and tricks of the trade** (purging bad writing habits and acquiring good ones)

Such a curriculum would drill heavily on audience/purpose and words in fourth and fifth grade, maybe introducing sentences toward the last few months. In sixth grade we'd review those concepts for the first few months and then spend the rest of the year on sentence writing. We'd start teaching paragraphs at the end of sixth grade, and then spend all of seventh grade reviewing what we've learned up until then. Rules and tricks is an eighth grade concept.

Does that mean the kids shouldn't be writing reports until eighth grade? you're probably wondering.

Yes, that's what it means. It will take that long to teach most students the fundamentals.

Besides, why rush kids into writing essays and reports? Do we really believe that assigning these projects in fifth grade (or earlier!) instead of eighth will help students develop better writing skills by high school and college? I believe we should postpone these types of projects and use the extra few years to teach writing one skill at a time, building as we go.

Concepts like *economizing wording* and *avoiding passive voice* are writing's equivalent of multiplication tables and memorizing states on a United States map. Those kinds of fundamentals are what this book is all about. For the next ninety or so pages, I'll do my level best to overload you with practical ideas that won't help your students' spelling, grammar, or creativity a bit—but will vastly improve the *effectiveness* of their writing.

Budding novelists need not apply. The kind of writing I'm talking about is the kind that gets its message across quickly and clearly, and gets results. That's what kids need to learn, because that's what the world—not to mention their future employers—will demand from them.

This morning I scanned the Want Ads in my Sunday paper. Here's a sampling of the jobs requiring "good oral and *written* communication skills:"

- **Hospital production assistant** who'll deal with packing slips, safety issues, and equipment maintenance
- **Executive assistant** responsible for screening phone calls, making travel plans, and performing other administrative chores
- **Income-processing clerk** to handle premium payments at an insurance company

Techniques for effective writing often seem to contradict what we teach about grammar and syntax. But so what? All of us routinely stretch the rules of grammar in our everyday communication, anyway. For example, we all dangle an infinitive now and then. (As in, "What kind of music do you listen to?" instead of the stuffy-sounding, "To what kind of music do you listen?")

We misuse subject and object pronouns, too. (As in "Who did you take that book from?" instead of the even stuffier-sounding, "From whom did you take that book?".) Why, we even mix up *may* and *can* every once in awhile when no one's listening, don't we? C'mon, you can admit it. (Oops! I mean, you *may* admit it.)

It's not that we don't know the rules. We simply exercise our option to bend or break them if it helps us get our point across. Yet we teach kids it's inappropriate to take these liberties when writing anything more formal than a phone message. Rules of grammar are supposed to aid communication, not hinder it.

While we're at it, let's demystify writing just a tad. Move it out of the academic arena and into the practical. Writing is not some mysterious talent possessed mainly by bearded, reclusive geniuses who sit hunchbacked at cheap typewriters, pounding furiously and stopping only to yank out an occasional less-than-perfect page and slam dunk it into the wastebasket. It's a life skill. Less like history and geometry. More like manners, wardrobe selection, and the ability to balance a checkbook. Those who do it creatively might be able to write for a living. But those who do it effectively can write for life.

# Chapter 1

# *Defining the Audience*

## *Who Are They and Why Are They Reading?*

"Who am I? Why am I here?" A politician spoke those words to a prime-time TV audience in 1992, and they've stuck with me ever since. They demonstrate the mindset of a presenter focused squarely on his audience and his purpose.

The speaker was Admiral James Stockdale, Ross Perot's running mate during the 1992 Presidential campaign. Stockdale uttered that somewhat famous line during a debate with his opponents, Al Gore and Dan Quayle. Instead of starting his part of the debate with a speech about the economy or foreign affairs, Stockdale chose to vocalize the question that he knew was on most viewers' minds.

I don't recall how Stockdale answered his own question. What I do remember is that his opening line illustrated the most important habit you can teach kids about writing: Before they start, make sure they know who's going to read what they write and why the person is going to read it.

We do this naturally when we talk, but that's because it's easy to see the person we're talking to. Their physical presence automatically tells us what to say and, more importantly, how to say it. Even in telephone conversations, we can visualize the person on the other end of the line.

# ▤ Out of sight, out of mind?

But writing is more anonymous. Unless they're writing a personal letter, kids generally start off with little or no idea what their reader looks like, let alone what his interests and needs are or what he expects to get from his reading. The result is usually writing that lacks clarity, focus, and purpose.

Don't let your students rush to start their writing assignments. After you've assigned the topic, assign a target audience and purpose, and get the class talking about them. A good question to ask the kids is: "If you were going to send this piece of writing to the one person in the world that you think should read it, whose name would go on the envelope?" Typically, kids will answer, "You." That's OK once in awhile. But be prepared to vary the audience when you give writing assignments.

Essays on complex subjects are a good place to practice writing clearly and effectively for a specific audience. That's because students tend to lapse into scholarly-speak when they do this kind of writing. Never assign an essay to your students without assigning a specific audience, too. If you want them to write conversationally, tell them their reader will be another student instead of an adult.

My seventeen-year-old showed me three essays she'd recently written for her European history course. Had her teacher assigned her an audience to write for, she and her classmates probably would have written much more clearly and effectively.

Granted, the subjects were heavy duty. They were analyses of the writings of three 18th century Americans of foreign descent: Ben Franklin; Puritan minister Jonathan Edwards; and Michel-Guillaume Jean de Crevecour, a French American nature writer.

But imagine if the teacher had said, "I want you to write a letter to your best friend about these subjects. Use the same common, everyday language you'd use in personal letters to explain the concepts. Do whatever you have to to make them interesting and understandable."

I'll bet (I hope!) my daughter's essays would have contained far less jargon. Instead of *exhibits many paradoxical views*, she'd have written, *contradicts himself*. Instead of *Crevecour states*, she'd have written, *Crevecour says. Valid meaning* would become *makes sense*. And so on. The whole tone of her writing would have been much clearer and more conversational.

Another example: Next time you assign a book report, tell the kids to write it for a first grader. Hopefully at least one student will remind you that first graders can barely read—which is exactly the point! The students will have to use much simpler words and sentences than they'd use when writing for . . . well, for whomever they usually write book reports.

They'll have to simplify their concepts, too. The *climax* of the story will have to become *the good part*. They might be able to get away with referring to the *theme* as *the moral of the story*. But even that well-known idea is likely to zoom over a typical first grader's head.

Other ways to vary the audience:

- Pair up a boy and a girl and have them write a report on a famous person for each other to read. (The person they choose to write about and the things they emphasize about that person shouldn't be the same as if they were writing for a friend of the same sex!)

- Have the kids write a report on how to win at their favorite video game—for their parents to read. (First they'll have to explain how to turn the game *on* and what all those control buttons actually *do*—none of which they'd need to discuss if they were writing for a classmate!)

- Have them write a report about their favorite vacation spot—but in two different versions: one aimed at convincing a classmate to go there and one aimed at convincing you to go there. (If the kids are thinking, the two versions will differ greatly. One will highlight restaurants and cultural attractions, and the other will feature a detailed list of junk food available in the hotel-room minibar.)

With a little imagination you can dream up plenty of your own audience variations. Expect to spend the better part of an entire class period talking about audience and purpose the first few times you give a writing assignment. After awhile, the discussions will go faster because kids will learn to visualize their readers faster. Getting a strong mental picture of their reader will help your students decide not only what to write but how to write it.

Conversation again provides a good example. Adults rarely use the same language with kids that they use with other adults, even if they're discussing the same subject. We even vary our language with different groups of adults. We tailor our words—if not the very subjects we discuss—to the people we're around. For example, would you make fun of a local political candidate if you were at a neighborhood cookout among friends who were working on his campaign? Not if you wanted to stay friends with them. Hopefully you'd do just the opposite: You'd bring up some interesting comment he'd just made on TV or a piece of legislation he planned to sponsor if elected.

You do this to be polite and engaging—to draw your friends into the conversation. Writing requires the same "audience-first" approach for the same reason: When we fail to tailor our message *and* our language to our reader, our reader goes elsewhere. Reminding your students of this is the first step toward helping them practice audience identification before they write. (See Figure 1-1 for two more fun ways to get this point across.)

## Pepsi vs. Coke

Advertising and public relations professionals are masters at writing for specific audiences. Their work is all around us, and it's a great teaching tool. These folks know that lots of different people will see their ads and commercials. But when they're designing an ad campaign, they focus on one target audience. Just by using the right words and images, they can make an ordinary product like soft drinks or toilet paper appeal to a certain group of people.

A good example is a Pepsi Cola commercial that ran on TV in the early 1990s. Pepsi's goal was to make people think that its product was a really cool cola for young people while its arch rival, Coca Cola, was a stale old drink for senior citizens. So, Pepsi showed a bunch of *really* old people drinking Coke at a party with bland elevator music playing in the background and everyone standing around like statues.

Then the camera flashed to the Pepsi party. It was full of obviously hip young kids having a great time dancing to some hot new tunes.

There are two reasons Pepsi used this humorous contrast of images.

## Figure 1-1 Fun Ways to Teach Audience-Identification

1. *Give your students a writing assignment on a general topic but geared to a specific audience of their choosing.* For example, have them write an essay about all of the different climates in the world, with the target reader being:

- A scientist
- An airline pilot
- A ship captain
- A prehistoric cave-dweller
- A fashion model
- A farmer
- A doctor
- A kindergartner

Before they write a word, make them list everything they know about their typical reader: age, gender, type of job or income, marital status, hobbies—as many data points as possible. If the kids are young enough (no older than fourth or fifth grade) you could even have them draw a picture of their typical reader—including their house, car, family, and any other key facts. Don't let them start until you're convinced they have a clear mental picture of their reader and of how to make the subject appeal to him.

When they're through, have them read the assignment out loud, and let the rest of the class guess who the typical reader is. See how accurately the class's guesses match the writer's target.

2. *Photocopy two articles from a Sunday newspaper.* One should be from the sports section (a typical story about a recent game, containing the usual scores and statistics). And the other should be from the fashion section (any fashion article will do—what's in for spring, the merits of wool . . . it doesn't matter).

Working with one article at a time, ask the class to make two lists side by side. One list contains everything they know about the *typical reader* of that article. The other contains each item of *information* in the article.

*(continued on page 6)*

*(continued from page 5)*

For the sports article, your list of *reader traits* might include:

- Male (*Yes*, I know women read sports articles. I said "typical" reader. No nitpicking, please).

- At least 10 years old (or old enough to want to read a newspaper occasionally).

- Interested in sports.

- Interested in the specific sport covered in the article.

- Interested in the specific team(s) covered in the article.

- And so on.

The *article information* list might include the winner and loser, the score, highlighted players or plays . . . that sort of thing. Keep these data points in the same order as they appear in the article.

Now make the same two lists for the fashion article. The list of reader traits will probably include info on gender, age, fashion-consciousness, and so on. And the article info will include designer names, colors and/or styles, maybe uses for the clothing. You get the point.

Spend a few minutes talking about how well the information matches up with the reader of each article. Then erase both lists of *article information* and tell the class you're going to rewrite each article for the opposite audience. Next to the fashion article's *reader traits*, make a list of the information you'd include for those readers in an article about the same sports contest. Would you lead off with the score and some highlights? Not if you wanted to keep your job at that newspaper! More likely, you'd include information about the colors of the uniforms, the materials, and the socks and shoes. You'd probably stick the score in there somewhere but certainly not in the opening paragraph. In fact, it might be in the last paragraph.

Play this one right and your class will have a lot of fun with it. More importantly, they'll never forget how important it is to pick a particular audience and write for it alone.

One is obvious: because its target audience is people who drink soda pop. Kids do. Senior citizens don't—at least not as much as kids do.

But there's a hidden reason, too. Soda pop is an inexpensive snack item that people generally don't take too seriously. In fact, kids (Pepsi's target audience) don't take much of anything too seriously. So, to appeal to them, Pepsi not only had to use the right images but also chose to make the commercial funny. The same commercial with more realistic old people (some of us *do* listen to popular music and wear jeans) wouldn't be nearly as effective.

Companies selling more expensive products—say, luxury cars—take just the opposite approach. Their target audience is usually an older person who earns a high income and takes himself and his car-buying very seriously. You won't see a lot of humor in Mercedes Benz commercials—unless the company decides to sell less expensive cars and target younger buyers.

You get the idea. There's no better textbook for teaching audience-identification techniques than the magazine ads and TV commercials we see every day. You'll never go wrong encouraging students to follow their example. Insist that they decide whom they *mainly* have to reach or influence before they write, and encourage them to banish all thoughts of non-target readers.

## Who'd read this ad?

To really get this point across, have the kids bring in some ads from magazines and newspapers. Start a discussion about the customer being targeted by each ad. How old is the customer? Is it a male or a female—or does gender even matter? Get the class also talking about who *wouldn't* be target audiences for the ads. For example, if it's an ad for a fancy, expensive restaurant, how would the typical McDonald's customer react to it? Would the ad make him want to eat . . . er, dine at the fancy place? Or would he clutch for his wallet and gasp at the high prices?

Once the students get the general idea, here's how to fine-tune their audience-identification skills even more: Have everyone in the class bring in an ad from the newspaper or magazine of their choice, but all for the same type of product—say, furniture. Then get them talking about the publication it came from and its typical reader. From there, focus on the ad itself: the

### Figure 1-2 How *Not* to Target an Audience

A good example of how not to target an audience is those photocopied family updates that some people send with holiday greeting cards. (I apologize if you're one of them. Maybe you'll change your errant ways after reading this.) The writers of these miniature family yearbooks seem to think that every single one of their readers—no matter how old they are, how far away they live, or how frequently they keep in touch—is interested in the same news.

"It contains something for everyone on our mailing list," explained one relative of mine who sends these things out every year. "Oh yeah?" I felt like saying, "Well if you want to write to your whole 'mailing list' as if it's a single, gender-neutral organism selected for his . . . er, *its* . . . conformance to a narrow list of demographic parameters, then don't be insulted if we all chip in and buy just one wedding present for your daughter."

You could make a nice writing assignment out of these one-size-fits-all family updates. Ask the students to write a few versions targeted at different members of a distant household: one for their closest friend in the household, one for the rest of the kids, and one for the parents.

kind of house that the target customer probably owns, maybe the kind of car, likely occupations or income levels, and other details.

This demonstrates to kids how you can write about the same subject to vastly different types of people. Cigarette makers are masters of this. They can take the same ingredients—tobacco and some tissue-thin paper—and make them appeal to two completely different audiences just by the words and pictures they use in their ads.

This process has to become automatic for students. You want to get them to a point where they start picturing their reader in their mind before you've finished giving them the due date for the assignment.

## What's my purpose?

Once your students know who they're writing to, they'll find it much easier to pinpoint their purpose for writing. Here's the question I recommend asking to launch this idea: "What will your reader *learn* or *do* after reading what you've written?"

The opening line of traditional wedding services is a great example to keep in mind during the discussion: "We are gathered here today to join this man and this woman in holy matrimony."

Is that an awesome statement of purpose, or what? Fifteen words—mostly one or two syllables apiece. Yet they leave absolutely no doubt what's about to happen. If you had to leave the church right after hearing that statement, you'd still know exactly what took place while you were gone.

For almost everything your students write, their purpose will fall under one or more of the following categories:

- Request

- Inform

- Teach

- Entertain

Let's look at each purpose individually. They're worth at least a couple of class sessions apiece. Don't try to cover them all at once.

## Tell Before You Ask

*Requesting* and *Informing*: These are closely linked. Informing, of course, is the same as telling. You're giving people information and nothing more. When you're informing, your goal is to present certain facts. What's the logical way to start that process? You guessed it: Make a list of the important facts you need to get across.

I've given an assignment I call "100 facts" to teach this idea. Have the kids list one hundred individual facts they can find about any topic they're interested in. It can be a person, a country, a world event . . . anything. One hundred is a good number because to compile a list that long, kids usually run out of important facts and have to tack on some rather unimportant ones. They also end up with individual facts that are related to each other.

That's exactly what you want. Now you can have them go back and reorganize the facts into logical groupings, and maybe even re-list them in order of importance. Of course, the order of importance can change with the audience. If it's a list of facts about the local shopping mall, then the location of fast-food restaurants and video arcades won't be as important to you as it will be to a seventh-grader.

Sounds a lot like the way we teach outlining, doesn't it? Well, it is—except it's simpler and, frankly, more useful. Outlining has too many rules. Kids get caught up in them and forget the original purpose, which is to organize facts into a logical order before writing about them.

After half a dozen or so "100 facts" assignments, the kids will have learned the value of lists for writing coherent, well-focused information pieces.

*Requesting* is an extension of that process. It requires you to ask for something *and* to tell people what they need to know before they decide on your request.

For example, say your students want to write their parents a note asking permission to join the school table tennis club. Step 1 is informing—listing all the facts their parents will want to know about the club. The list will look something like this:

1. *Cost is $50 for equipment rental and snacks.*

2. *Ten teachers chaperone—about one for every five students.*

3. *Games are every Thursday after school.*

4. *Need to be picked up at 7:00 P.M.*

5. *Need money by next Friday (check payable to Northern Junior High School).*

Insist that the kids leave out unnecessary words at first—even most adjectives and adverbs. Remember, we're shooting for clear, effective communication and nothing else. Besides, they can always add descriptive words later. That's the nice thing about lists. You can do all sorts of things with them—rearrange them, add more details to each main point, combine two similar points into one main item—you name it.

If the students' only purpose were to *inform* their parents about the table-tennis club, they could stop with the initial list and have an effective document. But to turn the list of data points into a *request*, they need to add a question, ideally right up front: *Dear Mom and Dad: May I join the table-tennis club this year? Here are the details.* And to make sure they get an answer, they should end the note by spelling out exactly what they want their parents to do.

Use words that leave no room for confusion. Make sure there's no need for the annoying and overused closing sentence: *If you have further questions, please let me know.*

Parents *will* check back if they have questions. So will any reader of any document. People don't need to be told that they have the right to clarify. Instead of ending the request with this trite statement, teach your students to close the way a salesperson does: by telling their reader what action they want, when they need it, and what will happen if they fail to meet the deadline. Including one of these do-or-die statements without sounding demanding or disrespectful is the single biggest key to making an effective request.

The good news is, it's not hard to do. The trick is for the *writer* to assume the burden of the consequences. Don't tell readers what will happen to them if they don't do what you want when you want it. Tell them what will happen to you!

> *Although the money isn't due for two weeks, there are only 50 spots available and it's first-come, first-served. So I really need to turn in the money by this Friday or I'll risk losing a chance to join. OK?*

A request without a deadline and consequences is just a wish.

So that's how to make an effective request: List the information to support the request first. Then plop the actual request on top of it (in question form) and wrap it up by stating how and when the reader should respond.

 **Put Information to Work**

*Teaching* also incorporates the elements of informing. If a student intends to *teach* with his writing, starting with a list is still a good idea. Only this time, instead of issuing a request, he'll tell his reader *how to use* the information.

That's what teaching is, isn't it? It's not just reporting information; it's helping people put the information to work.

An everyday example of writing to teach is the assembly instructions that come with toys. What's the first thing you see when you finally pry open those knuckle-busting boxes, wade through the sea of plastic bags and cardboard filler, and tear open the hermetically sealed booklet titled "IMPORTANT: Read Instructions Before Assembling"? Right, a *list* of parts—followed immediately by instructions on what to do with them.

If all you got was the list of parts, you'd be pretty frustrated, wouldn't you? "Wonderful," you'd probably groan. "They tell me what parts are here but not how to put them together." It's the written, step-by-step assembly instructions that teach you how to make the toy.

That's a good point to emphasize with students when they're trying to decide whether their purpose is to inform or to teach. If they want to *inform*, all they have to do is present the facts (ideally in some kind of logical order, of course). But if they want to *teach*, they have to explain what the facts mean or how to use them.

Multiplication tables demonstrate the difference between informing and teaching. Think about it: what are times tables, anyway? They're just mathematical facts. When we give students a times tables chart and ask them to memorize it, we're not really teaching in the true artistic and professional sense of the word. We're just giving the kids information. The real teaching comes in when we start working on multi-layered multiplication problems and long division. Now we're helping kids put those mathematical facts to use. Many schools still teach reading in a similar facts-first way. They start by *informing* kids about letters and their sounds. Then they *teach* them how to use that information to read words.

You can help cement this concept by making clear *your* expectations when you give writing assignments. If you ask for a report on manta rays, what you'll probably get is several sentences telling you where rays live, how much they weigh, and what they eat. If you want your students to write something more effective than that (and I hope you do, now that you've read this far!) then give a more specific assignment. For example, ask for a report that will teach you how to hunt manta rays, or how to keep a manta ray for a pet. It will force students to gather the same facts (probably more) but to present them with a clear purpose in mind.

For example, my ninth-grade daughter had to do an essay on "The Courage of Peter Zenger" for her history class. (Zenger, a German American, was a Colonial printer. His imprisonment on trumped-up libel charges led to some of the first legal definitions of freedom of the press.)

She listed many examples of Zenger's courage, but it wasn't until the very last sentence that she explained the meaning of all those examples: *Zenger's courage . . . showed people what a loyal citizen would do for his community,* she wrote.

And yet, that was obviously the whole point of the essay—to demonstrate the Colonial view of community obligation. Her teacher might have extracted this more effectively by attaching a teaching purpose to the essay: "I'm British and a loyal subject of the King's. I'm very confused about this idea of 'community service' that seems to be popular in the Colonies," she could have told the class. "Teach me what Americans believe is a citizen's obligation to his community. Use Peter Zenger as an example."

My sixth-grade son's Health teacher had a similar opportunity. The assignment: write two short stories, one about a good loser, one about a sore loser.

That's pretty fuzzy direction for a class of normal sixth-graders. "I can't think of any stories," one kid will whine.

"How long do they have to be?" another will ask.

"Do they have to be true?"

"I don't like sports."

The assignment could have been much more effective if the teacher had said something like: "I'm going out for soccer this year, and you're my coach. It's my first time playing a competitive sport against other kids. I want to show good sportsmanship whether I win or lose. Give me some examples that will teach me the difference between how a good and bad sport behave."

Here are some other write-to-teach assignments your class will have fun with:

- **How to clean a house** Facts will include a list of rooms, where to find the vacuum cleaner, and typical places where dust and dirt accumulate.

- **How to grow tomatoes** Facts will include the water and nutrient needs of tomatoes and how long it takes them to grow.

- **How to care for a pet puppy** Facts will include a puppy's growth rate and eating habits.

- **How to drive from the school to the writer's home** Facts will include a list of all the streets between school and home.

- **How to program a VCR to tape a movie** Facts will include the time of the movie and the location and functions of various buttons on the remote control. Give extra credit to any student whose directions are so effective that the VCR isn't flashing 12:00 when you're through.

That brings us to the fourth and final "purpose" for writing: to *entertain*. I put it last for a reason. I don't think kids should be taught to write for entertainment as part of a school curriculum. It's fine as part of an enrichment program for certain exceptionally talented kids who may want to be professional authors. But that's a very small minority.

This book isn't for them. It's for the vast majority of students who'll grow up to be salespeople, computer programmers, electricians, machinery operators, teachers, doctors, lawyers, butchers, bakers, and candlestick makers. "Who are they?" you ask? They're the people sitting in your classroom. "Why are they there?" They're hoping you'll help them learn to write effectively.

# *Getting Them Interested*

## *Simple Words Make Sleek Sentences and Strong Paragraphs*

The first sentence of any written document will either attract readers or repel them. But in order to write good *opening* sentences, kids need to learn how to write good sentences, period. What's the most powerful sentence you can think of? I can think of three.

Oops.

Fire.

Help.

Few sentences in the English language convey stronger and more recognizable messages than these do. And few better illustrate that "sentence effectiveness" comes from using no more words than necessary to say exactly what you want.

Word economy is one of the most important writing skills we can teach children. It's also one of the toughest for us to accept, largely because of inertia. We grew up learning that good writing meant sentences filled with lots of metaphors, clever sayings, and descriptive words of all shapes and sizes.

That's true if the purpose of the writing is to exercise creativity and entertain your reader. When we teach kids to write creatively, we want them to aim for the most vivid, compelling, descriptive imagery they can. We want their prose to appeal to as many senses as possible.

They earn high marks by writing of *frozen, white kamikaze crystals hurtling their stinging force into our windblown faces.*

But in everyday terms, that's just a *blizzard.*

And kids need to learn the value of using everyday terms in their writing. In fact, they need to learn that before they learn the long, descriptive version. We need to emphasize that the most important writing they'll ever do consists of simple, everyday terms gathered into tight, concise sentences.

When they learn the long version first, they grow up measuring writing effectiveness by word count. "How many pages does it have to be?" becomes the first question your students ask when you give a writing assignment. (Stop me if you've heard this one.)

 **How to Economize Words**

Here's a quick exercise to introduce the concept of word economy.

Ask the class to help you invent a picture language made up of geometric shapes. Ask them to assign geometric shapes to the words *garage, car,* and *in.*

The predictable responses (and the ones that work best) are a square for *garage,* a circle for *car,* and a triangle—usually a right triangle lying on its hypotenuse—for *in.*

Draw the three shapes on the board and ask the kids how you should assemble them into a sentence that means *a car is parked in the garage.* The best answer is a square drawn around a circle—that is, the shape for *car* inside the shape for *garage.* The first suggestion you get might be a sentence that uses all three geometric shapes in sequence, starting with the circle (*car*), then the triangle pointing toward the garage (*in*), then the square (*garage*).

Good! This gives you a chance to ask the class how they might shorten the sentence without losing the meaning. Sooner or later, they'll figure out that the word *in* is unnecessary if they simply draw the square around the circle—effectively putting the car into the garage.

You can lead the class toward two important conclusions with this exercise. First, it shows the value of thinking about word count as you write. Had you gone with the obvious three-word sentence and spent no time weighing alternatives, you'd have ended up with a sentence that was three times longer than it needed to be. Second, it lets you point out that the short sentence you ended up with means the same thing as the long one you started with.

Some students might argue that the finished sentence uses a word that wasn't part of the original language (a circle inside a square). That's fine. You can point out that this word isn't new at all. It's just a combination of two words everyone recognizes and understands. We combine words in similar fashion every day to convey unique meanings.

Time tested

Steering wheel

Telephone pole

Those are all single words in our mind's eye.

When you're ready to go a little further with the idea, have the students write a list of descriptive nouns or verbs whose meanings take a few words to explain. I'm thinking of examples like *speeding, gluttony, thicket,* or *parched,* but any word that conveys some intensity will do.

Next to each word, have them write a longer phrase containing several adjectives or adverbs that mean the same thing. Call it a definition if you like. For example:

> *Speeding* might become *weaving fast and reck-lessly through traffic.* *Gluttony* becomes *gulping down food and drink in large quantities.* *Thicket* becomes *tangled green mass of trees and underbrush.* *Parched* becomes *dry, cracked, and rain-starved.*

Then have them use each version in a sentence.

*The car was speeding.*

*The car was weaving fast and recklessly through traffic.*

See the difference between the two? Both represent good writing—depending on your purpose and audience. This takes some teacher imagination, but it's a great way to teach kids how to write with both clarity and creativity, depending on their purpose.

Your goal isn't to position either creative or effective writing as superior. It's just to point out the difference between the two and to help kids learn when and where to use each style. When the students are out to entertain someone—to set a mood and create imagery—you *want* them to use lots of adjectives and adverbs. But when their goal is simply to convey information or make a point—which is the case with almost all of the writing they'll do in their lifetimes—they should avoid unnecessary verbiage. If one word says the same as three or four, go with it every time.

Use adjectives and adverbs only if they clarify the message. And even then, try to replace them with a single, more descriptive synonym. For example, *snarled* means the same thing as *bared its sharp, wet fangs*, but it's such a strong word that in this case, the difference in imagery isn't all that great.

## A Picture Is Worth ...

Your next step is getting kids to practice word economy in full sentence form. One way to do this is with an activity I call "A picture is worth a thousand words . . . or maybe fewer." Have the kids draw two different pictures communicating the same information. One picture contains just the facts, and the other is embellished liberally with modifiers. For example, have them draw a picture that tells what today's weather is and another exaggerating the weather for sensory impact. Beneath each picture the students should write a sentence saying what the picture tells.

If today is hot and sunny, the first picture should contain little more than a drawing of sky and a bright sun. Maybe there's a melting ice-cream cone or a panting jogger in the background to portray heat. But that's it. The caption they write should be equally simple: *Today is hot and sunny.*

The second picture should be much more dramatic. The sun might be growling and breathing fire. The landscape might be brown and dry-looking, littered with animal skulls and withered plant stems. In the foreground, a man in tattered clothing crawls toward the fading image of a cool, clear pond. Vultures circle overhead. The accompanying sentence should provide

## Figure 2-1 Sentences You Shouldn't Teach

Let me tell you about a writing assignment one of my kids came home with early in the school year. The teacher had asked the class to write "a paragraph about something we're going to study this year." Not just any paragraph though. It had to be five sentences long. And not just any five sentences either. There had to be three declarative sentences, one imperative, and one interrogative.

That's a fine assignment except for one thing: it doesn't teach any useful writing skill. Instead it teaches the kids how to identify, define, and use certain kinds of sentences. If you're going to give an assignment like that, please don't call it a writing assignment. Call it a "sentence-identification assignment."

To make it a *writing* assignment, you need to specify an audience and a purpose. In this example, the teacher might instead have assigned a paragraph that

- . . . teaches a kindergartner something interesting about a topic in a sixth grade textbook.

- . . . uses an upcoming unit to convince a friend how much fun school is going to be this year.

- . . . tells the child's parents about a subject he's going to study that relates to their jobs or interests.

There's a place in education for teaching sentence terminology—stuff like, *declarative, imperative,* and *interrogative.* But it's not in writing instruction. I suspect we teach these formal terms and definitions more out of habit than out of their proven role in improving a student's writing. Think about it for a minute. Do you need to know the meaning of *CPU, bit,* and *DPI* to use a computer effectively? Do you need to know the difference between fuel injection and a carburetor in order to drive your car? If someone evaluated your computer skills or driving ability according to how many of these terms you could define, you'd probably be insulted. Well, that's exactly why you should leave formal terminology and definitions out of your writing lessons.

much more than a mere meteorological observation. *It was one of those scorching, midsummer shirt soakers that makes you want to escape to a sauna, just to cool off.* (I stuck in a lot of s words because they create a subliminal *sizzle* feel.)

Get the idea? If you're reading a novel, you expect a long, descriptive version of the weather. But if you're dressing for school or work and you have three seconds to glance at the weather report in the newspaper so you know what to wear . . . which version would you want?

Here are some more examples to get you started.

- **Simple picture:** What you had for lunch. **Embellishment:** Make your lunch look so appetizing that I'll want to buy it.

- **Simple picture:** What you're wearing to school today (just the articles of clothing—no descriptions of their color or style). **Embellishment:** The colors and styles of your school outfit.

- **Simple picture:** The state where you live (should be little more than a map-style line drawing, possibly surrounded by other states to give the reader some perspective). **Embellishment:** An inviting look at your state's most attractive cultural or geographic features.

- **Simple picture:** Driving fast. **Embellishment:** Speeding.

- **Simple picture:** Heavy traffic. **Embellishment:** A traffic jam.

If you're feeling particularly creative, here's a variation of this idea that you might like to try. I call it, "What am I trying to say, anyway?" Compose some long, descriptive, flowery sentences and ask the kids to shorten them without sacrificing meaning. Exaggerate the descriptiveness all you want. For example, you write:

> *He lifted and extended one leg, and then the other, through tangled lengths of trouser that seemed determined to confound his every attempt to catch the school bus on time.*

Then help the students shorten it to what you're really trying to say. Something like this:

He jammed his legs into his pants quickly so he wouldn't miss the school bus.

Another example. You write:

> To the untrained eye, it will appear as nothing more than black ink on white paper. But look more closely! Questions! Fifty of them ... each a straw-covered jungle-trap waiting to ensnare any unprepared Social Studies student who wanders carelessly into Room 228 tomorrow afternoon.

Students shorten it to:

> Tomorrow we'll have a Social Studies test.

Don't worry if your sentences sound phony and contrived. In fact, make them as flowery and pompous as you can. Part of the fun is letting the kids recognize the phoniness—and maybe even get a laugh out of it. As long as they fix them with more direct, effective writing, you've made your point.

If you're not up for all that creative sentence writing yourself, leaf through your favorite short story or novel. You'll find lots of examples (not because they're written poorly, but because they're written to *entertain* rather than to *request, inform,* or *teach*). Copy them onto the board and have the students rewrite them.

Most examples will be physical descriptions of people or natural phenomena. But try to find some involving actions, too. Here's one from a novel about Texas high school football, called *Friday Night Lights*, by H. G. Bissinger (HarperPerennial, 1991). As you read it, note the intense imagery the author creates. Think about how you'd rewrite the sentence if your purpose was purely informing instead of entertaining.

> The joyous swells of the band, with no note ever too loud or too off-key, the unflagging faith of the cheerleaders and all those high-octave cheers served up without a trace of self-consciousness, the frenzied screams of grown men and women as the boys on the field rose to dizzying, unheard-of heights—little was different now

*from how it had been almost forty years ago when a*
*young businessman had sat in this very stadium.*

Whew! In case you're wondering, that "sentence" contains seventy-six words. It's a colorful piece of writing. And no doubt it fully accomplishes the author's purpose (there's that word again). But what *was* the author's purpose? Obviously, it was to create a vivid picture in his reader's mind—a picture of a boisterous crowd gathered on a Friday night for what's probably the most significant event of their entire week: the football game against the crosstown, rival high school.

But suppose he wasn't a fiction writer trying to set a mood of frenzied town-to-town football rivalry for his reader. What if he was, say, a police officer on security duty at the game—writing a report to tell the night sergeant what he observed in the stadium at the moment the two football teams ran onto the field? The sentence would be much simpler and shorter.

*As the two teams sprinted onto the field, the bands*
*played loudly, the cheerleaders screamed, and the crowd*
*roared with excitement. It reminded me of my own high*
*school days.*

Not nearly as vivid, is it? A fiction editor would flag that passage and ask the author to create more imagery. But as an informative sentence, it's plenty effective. It tells the reader everything that was going on at the time. It's not completely void of imagery, either. It's just a lot less wordy. Had he written something resembling the author's original paragraph, his sergeant would have thought he'd lost his mind. Yet, in the business world people aim for an elaborate, often flowery style of writing all too often. They end up sounding ridiculous. And their writing rarely accomplishes its purpose, because the reader can't figure out the message. It's hidden beneath too many words.

## What is a sentence, anyway?

All of this is probably making you question your definition of a sentence. Good! That means I've accomplished *my* purpose, which is to point out that effective sentences come in all shapes and sizes. Depending on its purpose, an effective sentence may or may not conform to the standard grammatical definition of a *sentence*. Some English texts stress that a complete sentence has to have a subject and a predicate. The subject or predicate can be understood or implied, but they're there nonetheless.

Here's a little quiz to see how much you agree with that requirement. As the closing sentence in her book report, one of your students writes these exact words: *A great book for kids of all ages.* Do you:

A. Circle the words with your red pen and write, *Not a complete sentence. What is 'a great book for kids of all ages?'*

B. Circle the words with your red pen and write, *Great economy of words!*

C. Read right over it with no comment.

I hope you answered *B* or *C* (assuming, of course, that the book's cover notes don't contain words like *steamy* or *lustful*, which would render the student's recommendation somewhat questionable). But please don't tell me you chose option *A*. There's no need to demand that the student use more words to convey a message that you already understood just fine. To do so is to foster wordy writing. I guarantee it will make your student think to herself, "Well, *this book* is 'a great book for kids of all ages.' How come I can't call *this book* an understood subject?"

Did you ever think defining a sentence could be so confusing? Let's make it a little simpler. Let's call a sentence "any group of words that conveys a complete thought."

*Ouch!* is a complete sentence because if you read it or heard someone say it, you'd know exactly what it meant: "Something hurt that person, and I should see if they need me to help them."

*A big brown fox walking through the woods on a snowy afternoon in January looking for food because he hasn't eaten for almost two months* may or may not be a complete sentence. At first glance, it doesn't convey a complete thought. When you finish reading it, you want to ask, "Well, what exactly do you want me to know about this fox? What did it do?" And yet, it *does* convey a complete thought in certain contexts.

## Figure 2-2 Teach Sentences Before Compositions

Can you imagine teaching long division before kids have mastered their times tables? Or assigning Beethoven before your young pianist can play two-handed scales? Well, writing instruction has a logical order, too. Kids have to master the basics before we can expect them to handle anything more. That means spending plenty of time on the rudiments of good sentence writing before we ask them to write paragraphs, reports, or compositions.

I'm not talking about one or two lessons, either. To get your students' writing off to a good start, count on spending several months on the concepts in this chapter. Insist that they understand how to replace three words with one before they write their first sentence. Then spend a month or two analyzing and rewriting examples of good and bad sentences that they've clipped from magazines and newspapers.

When you think they're ready for some real sentence writing assignments, allow at least two or three additional class periods to review word economy and sentence power one last time. And when you finally turn them loose, make sure they know who's going to read their sentences and why. Give them sentences designed to convey a specific message to a specific audience.

For example, say you've asked the class to write a science report on hibernation. A particularly creative writer might open the report with a series of descriptive clauses—each ending with a period—that lead into the topic very effectively.

> *A big brown fox walking through the woods on a snowy afternoon in January looking for food because he hasn't eaten for almost two months.*
>
> *Squirrels scratching frantically into the ground beneath a pile of fallen leaves.*
>
> *An overfed, groggy-looking brown bear lumbering lazily toward a cave.*
>
> *There's no mistaking the signs. Winter is coming and the animal world is about to settle in for its traditional three-month sleep that scientists call hibernation.*

So let's not get too hung up on the strict, grammatical definition of a sentence when we evaluate kids' writing. Let's allow them to put a period, question mark, or exclamation point after a group of words if we're confident they say something complete. Especially if they do so in the overall context. Like this clause does.

Here's a fun, easy way to teach kids the power of itsy bitsy sentence-wannabees. Ask them to write ten sentences containing no more than two words. You should get answers like "Yo!," "No kidding?," and "Cool!" Next to each mini-sentence ask them to write another sentence with the identical meaning—but containing a visible subject and verb.

You'll be amazed at how hard this is. I'll bet most of the class winds up with long, convoluted sentences that no sensible person would ever utter in public. Some of your more clever students may figure out they can replace "Yo" with "You, there!" or "Hey!" But these don't count, because they have no *visible* subject and verb. (Understood subjects and verbs don't count.) Same with "No kidding." The phrase has no synonymous longer version. It carries a certain smug humor (as in, "No kidding, Mr. Street Vendor, a real Rolex for $20!") that you simply can't reconstruct, no matter how many words you use. And "Cool?" Forget about it! As an expression of positive admiration, that single word says more than any full-length sentence known to mankind.

 ## It's What You Don't Write That Counts

Now that we've broadened our definition of a sentence, let's look at what makes sentences good or bad. One of the best and shortest sentences in print comes from the New Testament. It describes Jesus' reaction after he learns about the death of His good friend, Lazarus:

*Jesus wept.*

The beauty of this sentence is how much it says with so few words. There are several sentences before it, describing where Jesus was when He learned the news, and who told Him. So, by the time the author has to explain Jesus' reaction, he doesn't need adjectives describing the look on Jesus' face or adverbs describing the sound of His weeping. They would serve no good purpose and probably would get in the way.

*Jesus wept* tells you everything you need to know. That's what makes a good sentence. Not just what you put in it but what you leave out. Sound easy? Well, it is . . . sort of. The trick is figuring out how much information is too much for one sentence. That's not an easy skill to learn or teach. There are no rules to help you. It's like trying to teach someone how far in advance of an intersection to apply the brakes. A lot depends on how fast you're going, the condition of the roads, the strength of your legs and other things.

In general, it's better to have many short sentences than to have a few long ones. If you're the kind of person who likes benchmarks, use ten. Teach students to vary sentence length around that number, alternating short sentences (fewer than ten words) with longer ones. Don't count words like *a* and *the*. And don't drive them crazy trying to cut one or two words out of an eleven- or twelve-word sentence that follows one with twenty-six words.

Where can students find great examples of info-packed, right-to-the-point, waste-not-a-word sentences? The best source I know is the TV program directory that comes with your Sunday newspaper. Have the kids read the little blurbs describing episodes of shows. Here are some good and not-so-good examples that I pulled from the "TV Channel Choices" that comes with my Sunday paper. Good sentences:

- *All of an owner's thoroughbreds win their races and immediately die.* (Makes you want to watch the show so you can find out why.)

- *Spike and Drusilla want to use a deadly demon to extinguish Buffy.* (Ditto.)

- *As a cop in 1979, Sam is haunted by the frozen facial expression of a woman murder victim.* (Makes you want to know how Sam acted on his curiosity.)

- *Murder occurs at an outpost where a mysterious chest found on the ocean floor is opened, unleashing a substance that could threaten humanity.* (This one's marginal, because it's a bit long and it uses passive construction: *mysterious chest . . . is opened.* But it conveys a complex subject without confusion. Notice, too, that it doesn't name any characters. Why? Because the main ideas are the mysterious substance and its potential threat to humanity.)

Not-so-good sentences:

- *Baseball player Gary Sheffield takes revenge against Max for his old nickname.* (Confusing. Whose old nickname—Max's or Gary Sheffield's? Here's a case where simply rearranging the sentence can greatly improve its effectiveness. *Max's nickname makes him the target of revenge by baseball player Gary Sheffield.*).

- *Jerry gets upset when a lame comic follows his act.* (What does he mean by *lame?* Does he mean lousy or crippled? If there's any possibility for confusion, use a more accurate word.)

Using those episode teasers as a model, why not have the kids write one-sentence summaries of their own favorite shows? Here's a chance for them to use TV for an educational purpose even if the show isn't about the South American rainforest or the mating habits of chickadees.

My ninth-grade daughter's science teacher does something similar: He has the kids write a single sentence each day summarizing what they just learned in class. What a great idea! He's helping them synthesize the day's lesson and practice an important writing skill at the same time.

Newspaper and magazine headlines are another good model for strong sentence writing. A good headline serves the same dual purpose as a good opening sentence: It not only provides information but it also makes you want to read more of the article. You can easily turn today's headlines into a sentence-writing exercise. Just scribble ten headlines on the board and have the kids make up an opening sentence for each article.

If you don't want to use real headlines, make some up. In fact, imaginary ones may be better. That way, your more detail-conscious students won't get stuck on trying to include real facts in their opening sentences. They can just contrive some.

You can also reverse the order—write the opening sentence on the board and have the kids write the headline. Again, use real or imagined opening sentences. Whatever works. Either way, you're teaching kids how to be aware of sentence length and word economy.

If you're lucky, maybe you'll find write-ups of the same news item from two different sources that you can contrast for your class. I came across just such an example while I was writing this chapter. The subject was a very controversial, local issue: the construction of a new middle school that our district needs to accommodate rapidly swelling enrollments.

There were several extended delays by the building contractor. And, as a result, instead of starting the year with the two middle schools we needed, it appeared we'd only have one for at least the first few months. The school district's solution: All middle-school students would go to the existing school. Half would attend class in the morning, and the other half in the afternoon.

Two articles about the problem showed up in my mailbox within days of each other. One appeared in our local newspaper and the other in a separate newsletter-type leaflet from our school board. Let's study the two versions and see what we can learn.

First, the headline and opening sentence from our local paper (Allentown, PA, *Morning Call*, 8/11/98):

## EAST PENN WORRIED SCHOOL
## WON'T BE FINISHED ON TIME

*About 1,500 East Penn middle school students will be squeezed into Eyer Middle School for double sessions this fall unless a substantial turnaround occurs in the construction of the new Lower Macungie Middle School by September 1.*

Very impressive writing. In less than 15 seconds of reading, even a newcomer to the area would know the facts of the story and how they're likely to impact his family.

Notice how long that lead sentence is: thirty-seven words—six lines of a newspaper column. It looks more like a paragraph than a sentence. In fact, it stands alone as a paragraph in the article. But it reads very smoothly. Let's dissect it and see if we can figure out why.

The first thing you'll notice is it uses small words that the eye can read quickly. Only five words in the whole sentence have more than two syllables. One is a number (*1,500*) and one is part of the township's name (*Macungie*).

Second—and even more amazing—is that the sentence doesn't contain a single punctuation mark except for the period at the end! I'll bet that didn't happen by accident. The writer probably composed half a dozen or more versions of that sentence before settling on the one that ended up in print. For example, the writer could easily have started the sentence this way:

> *Unless a substantial turnaround occurs in the construction of the new Lower Macungie Middle School by September 1 . . .*

But that would have required a comma after September 1. Instead she puts this clause at the end. Why? One likely reason is she wanted to give readers the "what-it-means-to-me" part of the article first. She knew that squeezing two schools' worth of kids into one building was the part that would impact her readers. But I'll bet she also was looking to create a faster-reading sentence, and she knew that a sentence this long would slow down considerably if she stuck even one comma into it.

Leaf through your own newspaper for examples of nice, clean sentences like this one. They make great teaching tools. Look for sentences that contain lots of information and still seem to read smoothly and effortlessly. Each morning write one on the board and ask the class to help identify what makes the sentence so effective—so informative and easy to read. These discussions create awareness of effective writing.

Here are examples of other reader-friendly words and phrases the news writer used:

- She could have said *approximately* but she chose the less pompous-sounding *about* instead.

- She wrote *squeezed* instead of the obvious but longer alternative *forced to attend*.

- She used five words instead of nine to describe the people most affected by the construction delay (*East Penn middle school students* instead of *middle school students in the East Penn School District*).

- She used five words instead of seven to highlight the problem (*unless a substantial turnaround occurs* instead of *unless the builder greatly increases his progress*).

None of these techniques by itself makes any great difference. But together they result in a sentence that says a lot with a little.

As a regular classroom activity, you can have the kids bring in their own examples of effective or poorly written sentences from newspapers and magazines. It's important to include discussion and rewriting in these exercises. If the students bring in examples of hard-to-read sentences, have them identify and correct the bad habits the writers demonstrated. If they bring in good sentences, discuss what bad habits the writers *didn't* demonstrate. Then have the kids rewrite the sentences using more cumbersome language.

That brings us to the school board's write-up about the very same school-construction mess. It arrived by mail on fluorescent fuchsia paper. The headline says:

## EAST PENN SCHOOL DISTRICT
## MIDDLE SCHOOL CONTINGENCY PLAN

OK, they got my attention. So I read the first sentence:

> *Based on the progress to date of the Lower Macungie Middle School construction, the East Penn School District is preparing to conduct split sessions at Eyer Middle School beginning on Thursday, September 10.*

Unless I had already known about this mess by reading the newspaper, I'd be really confused. Why? Well, for starters, go back and reread the first four words in the sentence. Since when does *progress* force you to change your plans? When I see a phrase like *Based on the progress*, I'm thinking something good happened. Aren't you? I guarantee you that a newcomer to our district—someone who just moved in yesterday and has middle school-aged kids—would think this note contained good news.

But the really confusing line is yet to come. It's the one that says . . .

*is preparing to conduct split sessions at Eyer Middle School.* What are *split sessions*? Does that mean the kids go to school, go home and then go back again on the same day? That's sure what it sounds like to me. Nowhere on the entire sheet does it say that students from both schools will attend Eyer Middle School until the Lower Macungie building is complete. You have to figure it out for yourself. Granted, it's a fairly obvious assumption for a reader to make. But our goal here is to teach effective writing that conveys information clearly, not just writing that *makes it easy for your readers to figure out what you mean to say.*

 ## The One-Sentence Report

Once your students have mastered the fundamentals of good sentence writing, you're ready to give them the ultimate writing assignment: a report. For their first attempt, give them lighthearted topics they can have fun with. Things like:

- How to win at your favorite video game

- The best baseball player in history

- Why female chefs are better than male chefs

Have the kids do at least half a dozen of these. Then you can assign subjects requiring more thought and research, such as:

- A summary of this winter's weather patterns

- How to do long division

- The causes of the Civil War (or some other historical event they're studying)

Oops! Did I mention there'll be a key difference between these reports and the ones you usually assign? Sorry. These reports should only be one sentence long. That's right, one sentence. Tell the kids you want them to write only the lead sentence of the report.

Give them a minute to pick up their jaws from the ground. (You can do the same right now. I'll wait.) Then explain that they're still expected to do all the research they'd normally do for a report. But all you want them to write is the lead sentence. It has to be compelling and informative—something that will give the reader just enough info to want to ask questions and read more. Ideally, it will contain one or more of the following:

- An amazing or unknown fact

- A question, riddle, or brain-teaser

- A summary of the main points

- A statement that provokes thought or controversy

You can take the assignment in one of two directions from there. You may want to collect the sentences and write follow-up questions beneath them. Then, send the kids back to answer the questions in writing. Effectively what you're doing here is giving them an outline for how to complete the report.

Another option—and the one I recommend you try first—is to sit with each student individually and do the rest of the report orally. You play the role of casually curious reader, asking the questions that come up after you've read the opening sentence. You can have the class play this role if you're confident it won't become an inquisition. No matter which option you choose, if the sentence doesn't spark any questions you have to make the student rewrite it.

What's the point of such an assignment? Well, think about it. The real reason kids hate writing reports isn't doing the research. Their biggest fear is how they're going to organize and present all the information—filling up those five pages you asked for. That anxiety is what causes writer's block. (See Chapter 4 for some tips on helping kids overcome writer's block).

So, let them put their writing energy into a simpler, more productive task. Let them focus on writing a single, opening sentence that will lead them and their reader right into the rest of the composition. They can try out various versions without the anxiety of knowing they still have to write five more pages. What's more, you'll have the comfort of never again having to say, ". . . as many pages as it takes to tell me all of the information you need to tell me."

# Chapter 3

# *Keeping Them Interested*

### *Eight Rules to Keep in Mind as You Write*

Here are eight writing habits that will help your students attract and keep their readers' interest from the very first sentence.

1.  Put the most important information in the opening sentence.
2.  Start with the word *you* as often as possible.
3.  Keep your lead sentence to twenty-five words or less.
4.  Avoid starting with a sentence that needs commas and other punctuation.
5.  If you wouldn't say it that way, don't write it that way.
6.  Don't write *Stockings were hung.* Tell your readers *who* hung them.
7.  Back up your writing with facts. Always.
8.  Never use a piece of paper as a weapon.

As you can see, these habits are not really complicated. Some of them are so basic that you may feel silly just reading about them, let alone teaching them.

That's where it will come in handy to remind your students—and yourself—that writing is just another life skill. It's no different from eating, sleeping, lifting heavy objects, or even working at a desk. To do any life skill well, you need to learn good fundamentals and practice them religiously. If you have kids of your own, you know exactly what I mean.

"Chew your food thoroughly so you digest it properly." "Don't eat a big meal right before you go to sleep." "Lift with your legs, not your back." And the ever popular: "Sit up straight." Writing lends itself to the same kind of nagging little rules. Let's take a closer look at them.

## 1. Put the most important information in the opening sentence.

The first few sentences of any written document are like a price tag: They tell the reader how much investment he'll have to make to get some benefit out of the piece. Only instead of money, it's the reader's *time* you want. Let him know right away that he's holding a true bargain in his hands. Give him the best information—the most important facts—in the first few lines.

This is a very hard habit to teach kids, largely because it seems to make no sense. "If I tell them the main stuff right away, why should they keep reading?" That's a common argument, but it's also wrong—on two counts. First of all, you can't possibly get *every* important detail into one opening sentence unless you make the sentence ridiculously long. So, readers know there's plenty of reason to keep reading, even if you've revealed most key facts right away.

But more important, when a writer plays hide-and-seek with key information, people lose patience and concentration. They have certain expectations when they start reading. A good writer meets those expectations right away.

That's exactly why I listed my "Eight Rules to Write By" up front in the first paragraph. Did that make you think you had all the information you needed? Did it make you want to stop reading? Of course not. In fact, had I made you leaf through the entire chapter to find my eight rules, you would have become frustrated. If I already know what you're hoping to learn in this chapter, why would I make you hunt for it?

News stories are a good example of the *main-facts-up-front* rule. They almost always tell you in the first sentence who won the game, what law passed, or what Hollywood star is getting married for the seventh time. The writers know you'll dig deeper into the story for more details, but they also know they'd better give you some meat right away, or you'll move on to the next headline. Go ahead, take a look at today's paper. You'll find very few articles that don't give you practically all the key information in the first sentence.

Have the kids clip out some newspaper articles and bring them in for discussion, too. Write the first one or two sentences of each article on the board and ask the class to help you underline each individual fact in them. You'll be amazed at how many you'll find. Here's one from the Local section of my hometown newspaper, the Allentown, PA, *Morning Call* (11/19/98):

> *At a sneak preview Wednesday night, Allentown Mayor William L. Heydt and 10 contest winners from Allentown flicked a switch and brought the thousands of lights in the Lehigh Parkway to life.*

It contains all five key facts a reader would want to know:

- **Who** (Mayor Heydt and five contest winners)
- **What they did** (gathered at a sneak preview)
- **When** (Wednesday night)
- **Where** (Lehigh Parkway)
- **Why** (to fire up the locally famous display of holiday lights)

To help your students practice writing key facts into their lead sentences, challenge them to write you a one-sentence summary—right now, right on the spot—of what they learned in their last class period, or what they did at lunch, or what they learned in their most recent telephone conversation with their best friend. (That last one ought to be good for some chuckles.)

If the summaries run true to form, they'll be missing at least one of the five Ws I listed above. Most likely the time element. When you ask the class to "Write me a single sentence summarizing what you learned last period in math class," a typical student will write:

> *We learned that when you're multiplying two numbers with more than two digits each, you have to multiply one number. . . .*

That gives you an opportunity to point out the importance of including *all* the important details, not just the ones they think their readers are missing. The sentence should start off:

> *Last period* in math *we learned that when you're multiplying two numbers with. . . .*

Skilled, experienced, professional writers break the *main-facts-up-front* rule often. But they know lots of techniques for grabbing a reader's interest without dumping a ton of facts into the opening sentence or paragraph. (See Chapter 4 for some examples and teaching strategies.) They also know when to employ those techniques—and when not to.

I'll wager that you don't have any skilled, experienced, professional writers in your classroom right now. So, for maximum effectiveness, kids should learn that the way to grab a reader's attention is by giving him what he's looking for—the most important facts—in the first paragraph.

## ◉ "My purpose for writing is ..."

Of course, students can't do that very well if they haven't decided what the most important facts are. That's why it's crucial to establish *and write down* the purpose of the document. I can't stress this enough. So many kids sit down to write a document with their heads crammed full of information and opinions but with no idea how to organize and present it. That's because we've been stressing *topics* and *form* when we make writing assignments.

I'll get into the whole issue of teaching correct forms for certain letters a little later. For now, let me just stress that *purpose* is much more important than *topic* or *form*. Please don't let your students forget that. In the first draft of any written document, make them state their purpose right up front. *My purpose for writing is to*

> *. . . let you know that our class treasury is $400 ahead of budget, so we can have our Spring Dance as planned.*

*. . . ask you for an interview for the restaurant hostess position you advertised in the Sunday paper.*

*. . . find out how I can improve my science grade this marking period.*

*. . . teach you all about the country of Venezuela and its contributions to the world's economy.*

Kids don't have to keep that boring opening. But the act of writing down their purpose will usually help trigger a good lead paragraph. Here's how you could transform any of the sentences above into a clean-sounding lead sentence with just a few keystrokes.

- *You'll be pleased to know that our class treasury is $400 ahead of budget, so we can have our Spring Dance as planned.*

- *How would you feel about interviewing just one more candidate for the hostess position you advertised in the Sunday paper?*

- *Can we meet Tuesday after school to talk about some ways for me to improve my science grade?*

- *Venezuela is one of the world's leading exporters of petroleum products, despite being located thousands of miles from the oil-rich Middle East.*

It may seem like common sense to lead off with your main point, but you rarely see it in students' writing. A typical junior-high student writing about a surplus in the class treasury would lead off something like this:

Dear Fellow Class Officers:

We started the year with a budget of $500 for dances and we spent most of it within the first four months of school.

First, our Halloween Costume Ball cost $400 instead of $200 like we planned. Then we got hit with a big snowstorm that cancelled our Christmas fundraiser, which was supposed to earn $500.

It seemed like we couldn't possibly recover.

Well, you'll be pleased to know that ad sales for the yearbook are 12% ahead of budget, giving us $400

more than we need to print the book. So, we can use
the extra money . . .

## ⊙ Out With the Old, In With the New

By the time the writer got around to the main message—way down there
in the last paragraph—many readers would be frustrated or bored. Why?
Because all the stuff in the first two paragraphs is old news.

Don't let students start off by rehashing stuff that people already
know. Make them report the new stuff right away. *Then* they can add highlights from earlier in the year to put it all in perspective. It's not a tough
skill to learn if you give the kids some direction and practice.

For example, suppose you asked the students for a one-sentence summary of last night's football game (or whatever sport). The sentence should
say where and when the game took place, what teams played, who won,
and maybe even who contributed a great play.

Here are some more events you could ask the students to summarize
in a single sentence. Look for the same battery of facts as in the sports report:

- World War II
- Today's lunch period
- Last night at dinner
- This weekend
- My most recent phone call

Make sure the kids exercise common sense with the *main-facts-up-
front* rule. If they're reporting really bad news—or if they're making a request
that will ruffle some big-time feathers—it's best to e-a-s-e their way in with
some less controversial information first. For example, suppose, as Class
Treasurer, a student has to tell her classmates that there's NO money for a
Spring Dance this year. A brutal, main-facts-up-front opening would go
something like this:

> *We can't have a Spring Dance this year because
> there's not enough money in the class treasury.*

Ouch!

That's fine if your goal is to upset everyone. But you want them to remember all the good stuff you did throughout the year too! So, a better way to start the report is:

> *This year has been exciting and unpredictable! Remember those great decorations at the Halloween Dance? And all the fun we had during the four snow days we had off this winter? Those are great memories. And I'm sure we'll have plenty more before the year is through. Unfortunately, a Spring Dance probably will not be among them. Those great times earlier this year cut deeply into our treasury . . .*

A fun practice assignment you could give on this concept is for the kids to write you a letter explaining why they didn't do last night's homework. The best letters are the ones that lead off with information about the educationally enriching activities the student *did* undertake last night. Give extra credit to any student who tells you when he or she actually will turn in last night's homework. They know that the real key to delivering bad news is telling you when the news will soon be good again.

 ## 2. Start with the word *you* as often as possible.

"You're right."

"You really made my day."

"You'll love what our principal just told me."

"Your comments on my last report card gave me an idea."

Feeling pretty good about yourself, aren't you? Maybe a little curious about what you said or did to get such positive results from me? Kind of wish there was more here to read, don't you? I'm not a bit surprised. Nothing grabs people's interest more than seeing their own personal pronoun in the first line of something you've sent them to read. The *I* forms of those four sentences are nowhere near as pleasant and compelling.

"I agree with you."

"I enjoyed what you did today."

"I just heard from our principal."

"I'd like to share an idea I got from your comments on my last report card."

See the difference? *You're* the focus of the first set of sentences. *I'm* the focus of the second. Which of us do you care about more? I know it sounds really basic, but please believe me: *you* is the best word you can start almost any written document with. Force your students to do it. Once they get into the habit, it helps to ease one of the greatest fears kids have about writing: how to start. If they already know that the first sentence should contain some form of the word *you*, they have an automatic, built-in, fail-safe starting point for whatever they're writing. They don't have to agonize over their opening line.

There's an added, indirect benefit to using *you* right up front: You force yourself to think about the impact your words have on your readers—how they might respond, concerns they might express, follow-up questions they might ask, that sort of thing.

Need a quick example of how kids can apply this rule in an everyday assignment? Book reports are perfect. Ask your students to address their critique of the book to a specific classmate. Instead of writing why *I* liked or disliked this book, have them write why *you'll* like or dislike it. When I'm reading your book report, what I really care about is whether *I'd* like this book or not. But you can't satisfy my curiosity if you're preoccupied with *your* reasons for liking the book. And that's exactly the message you convey (however subliminally) when you lead off a book report with *I liked this book because. . . .* Contrast that lead sentence with this one:

> *This book has an ending so exciting that you'll want*
> *to start rereading it the moment you get to the last page.*

That draws me in a lot faster. It tells me the writer isn't interested in just conveying *his* feelings about the book. He's taken time to anticipate what *mine* might be. I might end up disagreeing with him as I read on, but that's fine. At least the sentence made me want to read more.

It's not very hard to lead off with *you* when you're writing something for a specific person—say, a teacher, parent, or friend. That's because you know the person you're writing to. But you can do it when writing to more general audiences, too. The trick is remembering that your general audience is made up of individual people. Just pick one and write for that single person!

The best assignments for teaching this concept are those that force kids to write about themselves without using the word *I*. For example, have them write a summary of their day—addressed to their parents or brothers or sisters—without using the word *I* once. Or, have them write a letter asking someone for something, without using that word. It's perfectly OK to use *my, mine, we, us,* and *our* in these assignments, but make sure the kids use them sparingly. On the other hand, they should use the words *you* and *your* at least five times each. What you're shooting for are statements like these:

> *What do you need most after you've had one of those days when nothing seems to go right? Well, if you're like me, you need. . . . And today has been one of those days. You know, the school bus splashed water across . . .*

Or, in a request letter:

> *Do you have ten minutes this afternoon to talk about sharing the TV? Neither of us has to go without our favorite shows if we work this out . . .*

See? You know I'm talking about *me*. But I'm using *you* and *us* all over the place.

Here's another assignment: Have the kids write a letter to someone containing only questions and statements about things that are important to the reader. Examples:

- *You often ask what we can do to keep from being bored on our summer vacation. Well, you like animals, don't you? So, why don't we ask our moms if we can get a kitten?*

- *Your last piano recital was great! You didn't seem the least bit nervous, and you played that Mozart piece without any music at all. Amazing!*

Have them write the same kind of letter to:

- An imaginary company listed in a Help Wanted ad (*Your ad for a waitress sounds really interesting . . .*)
- People selling a car through the classified ads (*Want to find a nice home for your Chevy?*)
- A clerk who has to work in a store on a holiday weekend (*Your customers are happy to see you even if you're not thrilled to be at work.*)

This technique can be really helpful when kids set out to write a long report or a term paper. They're never quite sure who their real audience is. Yes, they know you gave the assignment. But they know their parents are going to read it. Maybe some friends and classmates will, too, if you end up displaying the best papers on a bulletin board.

That's the reason for some advice I offered earlier: Don't just assign a topic for your writing assignments. Assign an audience and a purpose, too. If it's a term paper, tell the students ahead of time who they should write for. If it's you, fine. A parent, a friend, the principal . . . whomever. Just make sure the kids sit down with a clear picture of their reader before they write the first sentence. That way they'll know exactly who they're talking to when they start off with *you.*

## 3. Keep your lead sentence to twenty-five words or less.

Write your first sentence as if it's the only part of your document that your reader has time to read. There. If you skip the rest of this section, I know you got the main idea. But my guess is, you're already curious enough to stay with me for a little while longer. Why? One reason is because my opening line sent you a hidden but compelling message. It said, "Hey, I know you're busy, so here's a bite-sized summary right up front where you can find it easily. There's plenty more good stuff where this came from. And I won't make you work too hard to find it."

The second reason you're still reading: you're probably curious about—maybe even provoked by—my suggestion that you keep your opening sentence to a given number of words. The scientific reason is because thirty to sixty seconds is about the longest a person can read something without his mind straying. You're competing with daydreams, jangling telephones, ambient noise among other things.

Think about that. You rarely can focus on any single subject for more than half a minute before your thoughts wander, however fleetingly, to another unrelated subject. If that's not an argument for snappy sentences, I don't know what is. Insist that students keep their lead sentences short—no more than twenty-five words, and preferably less.

The simplest way to get this across is to pass out some photocopied paragraphs from textbooks—ideally high school or college texts. Have the kids highlight all sentences containing more than twenty-five words (which may well describe every sentence in every paragraph), and ask them to shorten each one.

Obviously, you should factor this rule into your thinking when you evaluate students' writing. If you come across an exceptionally long sentence, flag it and have the student shorten it.

There's a common-sense part to this rule: a long sentence containing mostly one- and two-syllable words is usually better than a short sentence containing several big, obscure words. Which of these sentences is more readable?

- *Tracks that flexed too far apart caused Tuesday's derailment of a train carrying combustible liquefied petroleum gas in a Bethlehem train yard, a Conrail spokesman said Thursday.* (Allentown, PA, *Morning Call,* 2/12/99)

- *Moreover, a somewhat dialogical relationship obtains among the sections of the text.* (Lippman, Matthew. 1969. *Discovering Philosophy.* New York, NY: Meredith Corp.)

If I thought you'd buy the idea, I'd suggest you evaluate sentence length on the basis of syllable count rather than word count. But I won't push my luck.

## 4. Avoid starting with a sentence that needs commas and other punctuation.

Punctuation slows reading. Don't make your reader pull out of his driveway onto a stop-and-go city street. Let him zoom onto an empty freeway for the first part of his journey. Keep your opening sentence free of unnecessary punctuation. It's not as hard as you think. There's not a single punctuation mark (except periods) in the entire opening paragraph of this section.

I scanned three articles on the front-page of my hometown newspaper today. There's not a single punctuation mark in the opening sentence of any of them, either. The sentences aren't short, mind you. One contains eighteen words and the others contain twenty-seven and twenty-nine words. But the words fly by because the writers somehow avoided the need for punctuation.

It's one of those unwritten, unspoken tricks many professional writers use. They know that commas and other punctuation are like stoplights on a roller coaster, turning what should be a speedy thrill ride into a stop-and-go traffic jam.

You see punctuation-free lead sentences most often in newspapers, especially in late-breaking news stories designed to convey lots of facts quickly. But they're fairly common in magazines, too. At most, a magazine writer might use one or two commas in a lead sentence. Usually, they try to get away with none.

Leaf through your favorite magazines and check out the lead sentences in some of the articles. Have your students do the same. I'll bet most of these sentences are shorter than twenty-five words and contain few, if any, commas. Of those that are longer or that do contain excessive punctuation—I'll bet they're cumbersome to read and should be rewritten. (Yes, lousy writing does occasionally escape an editor's blue pencil.)

Excessive punctuation in a lead sentence is usually the result of a writer not carefully thinking through his purpose. Look at this sentence: *Tom Dithers, lead singer of the Boston Beans, based in Lessismore, PA, today announced he was quitting the band, which he joined in 1991.* Twenty-four words. Gets the main point across. But it's frustrating to read. It contains too many clauses, mostly because it contains too much information. Break it up into two sentences, with the first one containing the information that best achieves your goal. If Tom is well-known locally, then your goal is to announce that he's changing bands: *Tom Dithers today announced he's quitting as lead singer of the Boston Beans.* You can wait until the next sentence or two to mention the band's hometown and the year Dithers took over as lead singer.

But suppose it's the band, not Tom, that's most familiar to your readers. In that case your goal is to report a change in the band's personnel: *The Boston Beans learned today that their lead singer is stepping down. He'd been with the band since 1991.* You can still wait until the next sentence to report the band's hometown and identify the departing singer.

Your role in promoting this habit is one of vigilance. Look for excess commas and other punctuation in your students' opening sentences and make the kids rewrite those. Your goal is zero or one. More than one comma calls for a rewrite. You can also give an assignment focusing specifically on this skill. Ask the class to write a one-page comma-free essay on anything they want.

## Figure 3-1 Ten Things You Should Never Do in Writing

1. **Guarantee** (leave this to lawyers)
2. **Threaten or accuse** (another one for the lawyers)
3. **Apologize or admit guilt** (only do this if you have a plan for improving)
4. **Use profanity** (a sure sign of a simple mind)
5. **Remain anonymous** (a sure sign of a coward)
6. **Lie** (you'll get caught; count on it)
7. **Report unconfirmed "facts"** (even if you cite the source and warn the reader)
8. **Report or repeat rumors** (you now *are* the source)
9. **State the obvious** (you might as well call your reader a moron)
10. **Support an opinion with an opinion** (unless you're a film or music critic)

Or, have them write ten or twenty sentences, each containing at least four commas. To make sure they focus on the concept instead of the subject matter of the sentences themselves, have them write all the sentences about the same subject. For example, ask for one sentence each about twenty different animals; Or cars; Or movie stars. After you've read the sentences (and probably had some good laughs), you can have the kids break them up and rewrite them without all the commas. But you may not even need to do that. Believe me, it takes real effort to write that many commas into sentence after sentence. By the time the kids are through, they'll have a good feel for how much you can bog down your writing with excess punctuation. They'll be much better able to think and write in bite-size pieces.

This rule is yet another one you have to be careful with. It should work for you, not against you. If your students positively have to stick a comma or two in their lead sentences, let them go ahead and do it. But if you can train them to live without the commas, their readers will appreciate it.

## 5. If you wouldn't say it that way, don't write it that way.

When was the last time you used the phrase *in regards to* in a conversation? What about *utilize*? Or *assisted*? Unless you're doing an oral dissertation for a Ph.D., you probably wouldn't think of using stuffy-sounding words like these. Not even in formal conversations. Yet people write them all the time. Here's an actual sentence written by a person applying for a job at a company where I used to work. *I am writing to you in regards to the recent advertisement I read for the position of assistant marketing director.* What's wrong with writing, *I saw your ad for an assistant marketing manager?* Or *Your ad for an assistant marketing manager caught my eye?* Or *I'd like to apply for the assistant marketing manager job you advertised.*

That's what the guy would have said if he'd seen the boss in a restaurant. He wouldn't say, "I'd like to talk to you *in regards to* the recent advertisement I read . . ."

**Figure 3-2 Eight Common Boring Words and Phrases**

1. **In regards to** (sounds like you're addressing a judge)
2. **Allow me to introduce myself** (nice to meet you, Count Dracula)
3. **It goes without saying** (then don't say it)
4. **Basically** (Uhhh, like, heh heh, surf's up, dude)
5. **Just a quick note to** (everyone says it and it means nothing)
6. **Enclosed is** (I can *see* what's enclosed)
7. **Feel free to call if you have questions** (I'm certainly not going to wait for *you* to call *me* if I have questions)
8. **I am writing to you** (Really? I thought you were singing to me)

Scour your students' writing for awkward and stuffy-sounding expressions like these. Be brutal. You know what the kids sound like when they speak. To reinforce all of this, make them read their writing assignments aloud as often as you can. If their written words don't sound like something they'd *say*, make them restate the sentence orally while you tape-record it. Then play it back and have the student transcribe it. You'll be amazed how much more conversational their writing will become.

Reports and term papers lend themselves well to this activity. Those are the types of projects where kids most often lapse into scholarly-speak, especially in higher grades where they think the report sounds more authoritative if they use more and bigger words.

It may not be practical to do an oral reading with every composition by every student. But you should never let a writing assignment go by without selecting at least a few of the papers for critiquing by the class. Just be sure to spread the oral-reading around, so everyone gets their writing critiqued a few times during the year. (By the way, the act of having their writing critiqued helps teach kids at an early age how to remove their ego from the process. The ability to take criticism of their writing is the first step toward improving it.)

Of all the techniques that give writing a friendly, conversational feel, contractions may be the best. Which of these sentences sounds more like natural speech?

> *Mr. Lemming, you are my dad's best friend, and I am willing to babysit for you Saturday night if you cannot find anyone else.*

> *Mr. Lemming, you're my dad's best friend, and I'm willing to babysit for you Saturday night if you can't find anyone else.*

No contest. The sentence that sounds best is:

> *Mr. Lemming, even though you're my dad's best friend, there's no way I'm missing the dance Saturday night to babysit for your dorky kids. At least that's what my kids told me.*

The very purpose of contractions is to speed up the pace of communication. Why else would they even exist? They serve no grammatical purpose. They're a cosmetic-improvement tool. But they work! Encourage kids to use them!

Keep an eye out in your students' writing where contractions can shorten phrases and sentences. Circle them religiously. Do likewise when the kids are reading their assignments out loud. Remind the class to listen for words that could be shortened into contractions.

Don't let them use contractions unnecessarily, though. *You've lost your lunch money* sounds better than *You have lost your lunch money.* But *I was wondering if you have any lunch money* is better than *I was wondering if you've any lunch money.*

Another conversational-writing technique is to start sentences with conjunctions—*and, but,* and so on. Or writing incomplete sentences. Like this one. I know your instinct is to tell kids this is forbidden. And if it will earn you big-time criticism from parents, administrators, or the school board, well . . . only you can choose how you want to react to that. But the fact is, people start their spoken sentences with conjunctions all the time. Teaching kids that it's wrong to write that way seems a bit arbitrary.

**Figure 3-3 Six Things to Do Freely and Often in Writing**

1. **Praise** (there's no better way to hold an audience)

2. **Request** (people love to be asked for help, and they'll almost always say yes if you ask them properly—which I'll talk about in the chapter about Pro Writing Tricks)

3. **Offer to help** (make sure you expect no help in return)

4. **Advise** (preferably when asked; even then, stick with *I* phrases, as in, "Here's what *I'd* do." And remember, advice is just an opinion, so back it up with facts)

5. **Report facts** (just facts)

6. **Use contractions** (no one ever heard of a list of Dos and Do nots)

If a student has written a thirty-five-word compound sentence with the word *and* or *but* in the middle, for heaven's sake let him break the sentence in two and start the second one with the contraction. Those two short sentences are much easier to read than the long, grammatically correct one is.

After saying all that, I have one last bit of advice on conversational writing: don't let kids go overboard. For example, too many fragmented sentences make it hard for a reader to follow your train of thought. I always think of comedian Dana Carvey imitating former President George Bush: "Been there. Done that. Not gonna do it again," he'd say in that clipped tone. An occasional passage like that is fine in writing. But if you do it for more than a few lines, readers will start longing for a good old-fashioned subject-verb matchup.

Another example: if you're like me, you often litter your spoken vocabulary with useless expressions. I can get into a *basically* mode when I'm speaking. So I have to train myself to avoid that word when I write. It serves no purpose. Kids, of course, sprinkle *like* all over the place—as in, "So, like, we're at the mall and, like, Stacey sees this really, like, cool pair of shoes and, like, asks the guy, like, how much they cost . . ."

Kids shouldn't write it that way even though we all know they might say it that way! (In fact, they shouldn't even say it that way.)

If you sense they're using conversational writing to justify careless speech habits, pull in the reins. The trigger should be clarity and effectiveness. When the conversational stuff impedes the reader's ability to focus on, and understand, the writing, it's gone too far.

## 6. Don't write *Stockings were hung.* Tell your readers who hung them.

Chapters about the passive voice have been written in many language books. Statements have been made about how boring it sounds when the passive voice is used in writing. Tips are offered on how to avoid it. Handy exercises are presented, through which the ability to write in active voice can be gained. Yet the passive voice is still read by people every day. Frowns are formed on their . . . Sorry. I can't go on like this. And you probably can't, either.

The point is this: if you want your students to come across as total stiffs who can put people to sleep just by walking into a room, let them use *were told, has been gathered,* and other popular passive-voice pomposities liberally in their writing.

Awareness is the key to eliminating passive voice. And a good way to create awareness is to have your students write in passive voice until they're sick of it. I suggest a two-step approach to this. As a first step, make up twenty active-voice sentences on your own that the kids can rewrite in passive voice. Your sentences should say something like, *Mom is serving us dinner,* so the kids can rewrite them to say, *We are being served dinner.*

Another example: your sentence says, *The cat ate the mouse.* Rewritten passive-voice version says, *The mouse was eaten.* (Even if the rewritten version says, *The mouse was eaten by the cat,* it's still passive voice.)

Once students grasp the idea, reverse the process. Let the kids make up their own *passive*-voice sentences and rewrite them correctly in *active* voice. I recommend they write twenty sentences every night for two weeks. Or have them turn in one hundred sentences at the end of each week for two weeks. That way you can check them all at once.

Make sure they write the active-voice version right next to the passive one. (And by the way, don't be surprised if several kids mistakenly write two active-voice sentences next to each other, thinking one is passive. That should only convince you that you do, indeed, need to increase their awareness of the difference!)

## 7. Back up your writing with facts. Always.

I've seen lots of good writing teachers emphasize the difference between opinion and fact. But their lessons typically fall a bit short. Kids come away from those classes thinking that it's OK to put their opinions in writing as along as their reader knows it's an opinion.

Wrong. It's only OK to put your opinion in writing if you back it up with facts. An opinion that's not backed up with facts is called gossip. If kids are going to put something in writing, they need to either back it up with facts or—at the very least—tell their readers where they learned it. If they can't or won't do these things, I tell them they're guilty of gossiping—and no one likes a gossip.

Oral gossip is bad enough. But it becomes especially troublesome when you write it down, because people tend to attach more authority to written words. That's because most people realize you can get away with *saying* almost anything. You can always claim the words came out wrong, or the listener misunderstood you, if someone objects to something you said. But you'd better have your facts straight before you put something in writing. Because if people object to something you wrote . . . well, it's right there in black and white. (Did you notice I just started two consecutive sentences with conjunctions?)

Kids face countless opportunities to use the *back-it-up-with-facts* rule in everyday life. Maybe you've asked them to recommend a certain student for classroom representative. Or maybe their best friend has asked them which of two movies they liked best. Whatever the subject, kids need to practice offering opinions with facts to support them. To do otherwise is insulting and sometimes sneaky. It tests a reader's patience and it abuses their trust. I start questioning a person's motives when they dangle too many opinions in thin air with no visible means of support. "What are the facts?" I wonder to myself. "Is he hiding them? Or are there no facts to begin with?"

It's much better to present the facts and let readers draw their own conclusions than to present the conclusions and expect readers to fill in the facts.

## ⊙ "Caution: Opinion Ahead"

Adjectives and adverbs can be key indicators that it's time to include some facts. That's especially true if those adjectives and adverbs are in comparative or superlative forms—that is, when kids don't just say "you give a lot of homework" but "you give *more homework* (comparative) than my teacher last year and the *most homework* (superlative) of any teacher in the school."

Statements like those scream for a chart showing the actual number of homework assignments made by the entire faculty over the past few years. Yet I'm amazed at how often people make such comparisons in writing and boldly expect their reader to accept them on faith alone. Don't let kids jeopardize their credibility by spouting opinions without presenting information to back them up. Make them think like lawyers and develop air-tight cases before they go to court.

To drive this skill home, consider adding a little twist to conventional book reports, term papers, and essays. Instead of asking students to just write about the topic, ask them to write about it and then offer an opinion about it. Lots of teachers already do this with book reports. They ask kids to include a section on why they liked or disliked the book. You can do the same with term papers and reports, no matter what the subject. Whether it's a country, an animal, a person . . . whatever. Just ask the kids to add an opinion section at the end.

You'll need to help them focus this, of course. For example, if the report is about a person—say, a scientist or a sports figure—the students can give their opinions on how that person's accomplishments rank among his peers. If it's about a country, the students can say whether they think the United States should be friendly or unfriendly toward that country. Or they can give their opinion on whether the country would be a nice place to live. And so on.

Your job isn't to agree or disagree with the opinion. It's simply to make sure the students support their opinions with facts rather than with more opinions. When you evaluate this part of the assignment, try to phrase all of your criticisms in the form of open-ended questions—that is, those that can't be answered yes or no.

- Where did you learn this?
- How many people use light bulbs today compared with the number using telephones?
- Who are the top home-run hitters among all left fielders?
- What else besides the warm climate would make Borneo a nice place to live?

## 8. Never use a piece of paper as a weapon.

Suppose someone sent you a nasty message by tying a note to a rock and throwing it through your window at your head. Teach your students to keep that image in mind next time they want to dash off an angry letter. I don't care who it is or how badly they deserve to be lambasted, it never makes sense to put anger in writing. Save your nasty words for a good old-fashioned argument. But never, ever, *ever* send them in written form.

There's something about written anger that makes it unforgivable and unforgettable. It's as if you're saying: "I'm so certain that these bitter, insulting words reflect my true feelings now and forever, that I'm willing to attach them to a stone and throw them through your living room window, if necessary."

The temptation to let fly in writing is especially great when you've just been on the receiving end of unfair criticism or rumors. My computer disk drive is full of vicious, angry letters and memos that I've never even printed out, let alone mailed. The targets have been neighbors, co-workers, my boss, my wife (Oops! Just kidding, honey). Sometimes I write them and then delete them. But just as often, I keep them on file so I can reread them or add to them when the spirit moves me. It's great therapy. But printing and mailing them is bad business—personally or professionally.

The reason is simple: When people read angry writing, all they remember is the anger. The message gets lost. (Just like hitting someone with a note tied to a rock. All they'll remember is getting hit with the rock.)

## Figure 3-4 Four Written Statements That Will Calm an Angry Person

1. You have a right to be angry.

2. There's no excuse for what I did, but I do owe you an explanation.

3. Thanks for your patience and understanding.

4. Please let me start fresh and show you I can do better.

## ◎ How to Write When You're Angry

So, what should you teach students to do when they want to write someone an angry letter? Teach them to focus on their real purpose—the thing that will make the anger go away. The best way to teach this skill is by assigning *before* and *after* letters.

Start with a discussion. Ask the class to tell you about a time they got really angry at someone. Maybe it was another student who cut into the line at lunch. Or maybe it was their parents for grounding them unfairly. Tell them to write that person a letter saying just how angry they are. Encourage them to vent as much as they want. When they're finished, read some of the letters aloud, if you want. Let everyone have a few laughs at the more creative expressions of anger and vengeance you've probably received.

Now comes the tough part—the part that'll teach them to think like writers instead of angry people: ask them what it would take to calm their anger. "What would the offender have to do to fix things and earn your forgiveness or friendship?" Guide them toward realistic answers that fix the problem ("I think the rude kid should apologize") rather than just providing an outlet for the anger ("I'd like to beat the crap out of him").

Once they've identified the fix, the letter becomes nothing more than a request. If you remember from Chapter 1, a request is really just a list of facts with an ask on top of them and a consequence at the end. You direct the consequence at yourself, though, not at the person reading the letter.

So have the class rewrite their angry letters as request letters. Remind them what they're actually doing here: "Remember, you're now asking for a favor from someone. So you have to approach this the way you'd approach anyone you wanted a favor from. You have to be calm and maybe even a little humble." You'll be amazed at how different these letters sound from the angry ones they wrote at first.

Try this technique yourself, first, if you want to get a feel for it. Write an angry letter to someone and then rewrite it as a simple request that they fix what they did to anger you. The hardest part about the second letter isn't writing it. It's getting into the right frame of mind—zeroing in on your purpose instead of your anger.

## ◉ Anger and Index Cards

A more elaborate but equally effective way to teach anger-writing is with 3 x 5-inch index cards. Have the students write their angry letters, then copy each individual sentence onto its own card. As they review the sentences one at a time, they'll end up discarding some and rewriting others in softer language. When they're through, they can just reassemble them into a more digestible letter.

Here's how it might work in real life: Suppose you've divided the class into groups to work on a project. In one of the groups there's a student who insists on tattling to you every time he thinks the group has ignored one of his ideas. (I'm sure things like this never happen in your classroom, but humor me.) The rest of the group would like to write him a letter saying:

> *How come you're always crying to the teacher*
> *every time you don't get your own selfish way? Grow up*
> *or get out of our group!*

That's exactly what they should write. But then they should copy those two sentences onto separate sheets of paper, and work on softening them up. Immediately they'll realize there's no way to rewrite sentence number two—*Grow up or get out of our group!*—in softer language. Its message is all anger and no substance. It offers the offender no alternative. He can't quit the group, because he didn't join it in the first place. The teacher put him there. The students should throw out that sentence.

When they read the first sentence—*How come you're always crying to the teacher every time you don't get your own selfish way?*—they'll see that it says two things.

1. *Tattling to the teacher is no way to build trust and comm*

2. *You're selfish.*

Uh oh. Message No. 1 (*Tattling to the teacher*) works OK. But Message No. 2 still won't fly. You don't encourage cooperation and creative thinking among your group members by labeling someone *selfish*. What the students really want to say is:

> *Sometimes you come up with ideas that just won't work, and you have to learn to accept that. It happens to all of us.*
>
> *And sometimes your ideas seem good, but we can't use them, because we don't have enough time or money (or whatever). Maybe you should talk to your parents or one of our group members individually before you bring them in front of everyone.*

Once they get to that point they can write a note that's not only free of angry language but that actually helps the classmate and the group.

Can I guarantee that the tattler won't get angry even after reading this softer letter? Of course not. People get angry when you tell them there's cabbage stuck between their teeth (as if the alternative—*not* telling them and letting them walk around all day with it stuck there—would have been less insulting). But tact works a lot better than anger does. Besides, spending all that time writing out individual sentences on pieces of paper might at least calm the kids down. It's like counting to ten before you blow your stack during an argument.

# In Case of Emergency!
## How Professional Writers Tackle Their Toughest Challenges

Professional writers typically aren't very creative. Does that surprise you? It's true. I've hired and trained many of them as book and magazine editors. Their vocabularies usually aren't huge and scholarly, either. And they don't routinely flavor their sentences with catchy metaphors and powerful adjectives. Nor are they well-versed in the technical terminology of our language. Lots of them can't even tell an appositive from an expository transition. (Come to think of it, neither can I.)

What they can do well is convey information in logical, step-by-step order so their reader fully understands it. That's the same skill your students will need when they grow up and get jobs. They'll need to write memos, sales letters, policy booklets, responses to customer questions, and—of course—they'll need to write e-mail. (If ever a new technology screamed for re-emphasis on writing skills, it's e-mail.)

Here are some of the tricks professional writers use to write better, faster and more clearly.

### Overcoming "Writer's Block"

Let's debunk a myth right now: There's no such thing as writer's block. What we've come to call writer's block is a fable created by people who think everything you write has to be clever. Next time your students think they're suffering from a bad case of writer's block, tell them to just write . . . anything. Encourage them to back off the creativity throttle and write what they're thinking. Tell them not to worry about how clever it sounds. Let them just write it in the simplest, most mundane words that come to mind.

And tell them not to worry about how to get started. One trick professional writers use when they can't think of a good opening sentence is to start writing in the middle of the piece. They step back from the assignment and think about all the topics and subtopics they'll eventually have to include in it. Then they just pick one where the words seem to come fairly naturally, and they start writing.

Encourage your students to do the same thing if they're struggling with their lead sentence. Tell them to write about the first topic that comes into their heads (within the assignment, of course), no matter how insignificant. If they're writing a book report, maybe it's some crazy habit that the lead character had. A term paper about a foreign country? Write about its national motto or the color of its flag.

Now, suppose they've written everything *but* the first sentence or paragraph—and they're still "blocked." Tell them to write the conclusion instead. They can even start with the words, *In conclusion* . . . if they want. (If they've already written the conclusion, tell them to write another one!) Chances are, the sentence or paragraph they end up with will work just as well if they use it as an opening sentence.

Likewise, if the kids are having trouble writing an ending for their assignment, tell them to end it with a new version of the opening sentence. That's right: just rewrite the opening sentence and put it at the end of the story. (OK, maybe they'll want to adjust the wording so it sounds a little different but means the same thing.) If they want, they can set it aside and come back to it later. Chances are they'll think of another point or two to add, and pretty soon they'll have an entirely different sentence.

## Are you talking to me?

"Live quotes make great opening sentences."

I'll bet you're wondering who said that, aren't you? Well, it was no one famous. Just me. But the quotation marks got your attention, didn't they? That's because readers are naturally drawn to anything that departs from plain old prose. Quotation marks signal to a reader that someone else has just joined the conversation.

Professional writers often use quotes in their opening sentence or paragraph—especially with feature stories (as opposed to straight news reports), where the characters and concepts are key elements. It doesn't work as well with hard-hitting, just-the-facts news articles, because readers usually are looking for the *who, what, why, when,* and *where* right up front.

Live quotes make especially good leads for book reports. If a student is having trouble starting his book report, encourage him to look for a quote from a main character. The ideal quote is one that summarizes a main message of the book or sets the stage for a key scene. Take this example from *Dave Barry's Complete Guide to Guys* (Random House, 1995):

> *My feeling is that the world would be a much bet-*
> *ter place if more males would stop trying so hard to be*
> *Men and instead settle for being guys.*

Or this one from Henrik Ibsen's famous play, "An Enemy of the People":

> *The majority is never right until it does right.*

Despite coming from vastly different types of writing, either of those quotes would make a great lead for a book report. They get you interested in the book, the speaker, and—by association—the book report, itself. Leadoff quotes work well for biographical reports, too. Most famous people have made at least one noteworthy comment that you can use as a starting point for a report.

The quote could be real ("Ask not what your country can do for you. Ask what you can do for your country."). Or it can be part of folklore ("Father, I cannot tell a lie. It was I who cut down the cherry tree."). Either way, as a writer, you now have a built-in transition to a description of your subject and his or her life.

Kids can use this technique with most any kind of composition. A term paper about a foreign country? Lead with a quote from its most famous leader or cultural figure. An essay about a social issue? Lead with a quote from someone who's spoken out on the subject in public.

Even in the body of the text, quotation marks are a time-tested attention getter. They immediately pique your reader's curiosity. "Hey, someone's talking here. I wonder who it is?" they'll think to themselves.

What if the students don't have a real, live quote available? One option is to make one up—like I did in the first paragraph of this section. They have to be careful, though. There are two rules for using imaginary quotes:

- Don't do it in a piece of writing that your reader expects will contain live quotes, such as a news story or a biographical report. To do so is deceptive and will hurt your credibility.

- Immediately identify the quote as imaginary. Again, if you go back to my imaginary quote at the beginning of this section, you'll notice I immediately told you it was made up.

Here's another example of how to use an imaginary quote as a lead sentence. Say the assignment is a composition about summer vacation activities. A student could start off like this:

> *"So much vegging, so little time." That was my first thought as I walked down the stairs to breakfast on Monday, June 10, our first day of summer vacation.*

But you wouldn't dare let kids use an imaginary quote like that if the assignment was to write about their best friend's summer vacation. A reader might easily expect to see a quote from the best friend in the first sentence.

The best way to help students learn this technique is to make it part of an assignment. Have them pick five quotes from a story or book that best describe the main character's outlook on life. Or have them bring in newspaper articles containing lots of live quotes and discuss how they might rewrite the articles with one of the quotes as an opening sentence.

## ⁞⁞⁞ Opening With a Question

Another reader-luring trick that professional writers use is to ask a question right up front. The best leadoff questions take the form of riddles or brain-teasers. For example:

> *What famous inventor of the electric pen and holder of more than 1,000 patents had only three months of formal education?* (Good opening line for a biograph-ical report about Thomas Edison.)
>
> *How are airplanes and apples related?* (Famous gravity-discoverer Sir Isaac Newton wrote some of the first known scientific papers about modern aerodynamic theory.)

On second thought, that airplanes-and-apples example may be more cutesy than it needs to be. You could get the same effect simply by writing:

> *Although Sir Isaac Newton is famous for teaching us about gravity, did you know that he also contributed to the invention of airplanes?*

It's a little wordy, but it's still interesting enough to draw the reader in.

A leadoff question might also be aimed at invoking empathy. You could almost write the rest of these two articles yourself:

- *Have you ever wanted to pound your alarm clock into a pile of plastic shrapnel?*
- *Is there anything worse than being betrayed by a friend?*

I discovered a great leadoff question in an airline magazine. It was in an article about a theater group whose plays were aimed at changing peo-ple's perceptions about the handicapped. The article led off like this:

> *How many times have you seen someone and immediately leapt to a stereotype on the basis of race, gender, ethnicity, or physical condition?*

The only thing wrong with this powerful lead is that many people probably never read it. That's because it's not in the article's opening paragraph but instead is buried in the second paragraph. Even worse, the writer preceded that sentence with a much longer one packed with unnecessary details. Here's the actual lead as it appeared in the magazine:

> In a world full of pretension, one in which we often fall prey to judging worth by a label, it is both humbling and refreshing to be reminded that people usually are infinitely more complex than a first impression may convey.
>
> How many times have you seen someone and immediately leapt to a stereotype on the basis of race, gender, ethnicity, or physical condition?

This writer would have been so much better off if he'd used his lead-off question where it belongs: at the front of the article. He obviously knew that asking a question is a good way to draw your reader into your writing. Unfortunately, he waited so long to ask it that he probably lost half of his potential readers.

One danger of leading with a question is stating the obvious. The most common example is sales letters whose opening line goes something like this: *Wouldn't you love to save $500 a month on your credit card bills?* Is there anyone on the planet who'd answer "No"? Leadoff questions with blatantly obvious answers don't intrigue readers; they insult them. Professional writers keep a sharp eye out for creampuff questions like that. When they spot one, often they simply turn the question into a statement: *Here's how to save $500 a month on your credit card bills!*

Another risk of using leadoff questions is that your reader might not answer the way you expect. Occasionally I get letters asking, *Is your home losing value because of old-fashioned windows?* They want me to respond with an urgent request for more information. But my home is only six years old. I'll toss that letter without reading another word. But if they'd started with a statement: *Learn how new windows can pay for themselves with increased home value!*, I'd probably keep reading. I'd be no more likely to buy from them *now*, but at least they'd get me thinking for the future.

Here's a quick, easy way to help students use leadoff questions properly: have them research a topic of your choosing and write twenty questions designed to spark their classmates' curiosity about the subject. The subject should be broad, like these examples:

- Transportation methods around the world

- Inventions that have changed history

- Foods that heal

- Earth's amazing geography

- The Bill of Rights

- How the human body works

- Nature's most powerful forces

Give everyone in the class the same source of information on the subject. Maybe it's an article from a magazine, or a long entry from an encyclopedia, or a printout of something you downloaded from the Web. Tell the students to highlight all of the fascinating or surprising facts in the article, and then to translate those facts into questions. Two examples:

> *What names for parts of our bodies come from ancient terms for 'little mouse' and 'little acorn'?* (The answers are *muscle* and *gland*, respectively, which I learned from reading the encyclopedia entry for *anatomy*.)

> *Do you know there's a part of the Pacific Ocean deep enough to hold Mt. Everest?* (No, but if you hum a few bars I'll try to fake it. . . . But seriously folks, at 5.5 miles high, Mt. Everest would easily fit into the Mariana Trench, which is 6.7 miles deep. I learned that by looking up *Pacific Ocean*.)

Have students put the questions in order of highest to lowest reader interest. At the top of the list would be the most compelling questions—those they think would be most captivating to their intended audience. These are the questions they'd definitely use if they were writing a whole report on the subject. At the bottom would be questions that make poor leads because they're too obvious, complicated, or insignificant. Discuss the list of questions in class. Chances are, only three or four make really good lead sentences.

Numbers are also great attention getters in an opening sentence. Professional writers use this trick often. They know you start forming a mental checklist as soon as you encounter a number. You keep reading to fill it out.

- *"Three things can happen when you pass, and two of them are bad," said famous Ohio State football coach Woody Hayes.* (Even a non-football fan wants to keep reading to find out what those three risks are.)

- *Investing in the stock market can be fun and rewarding if you follow five basic rules.* (Tell me you wouldn't immediately start scanning the article for the five rules!)

Encourage students to use this technique if they're having trouble organizing their thoughts before they write. It's especially effective when you want them to summarize what they've learned from a reading assignment:

- *The Industrial Revolution resulted directly from two forces merging in America's economy.*

- *Five things can happen to a falling drop of water before it reaches the ground.*

- *Polonius, Lord Chamberlain, gave nine bits of advice to his son, Laertes.*

All of this explains why you often see numbers in headlines and magazine cover blurbs. Next time you're in a convenience store or supermarket, stop by the magazine rack and scan the covers. I'll bet almost every single one has a blurb or two with a number in it:

- Five Ways to Improve Your Sex Life

- Three Keys to Better Health

- Seven 'Must-Have' Fashion Accessories

Speaking of headlines, another time-tested technique of professional writers—actually, it's more of a rule—is to *always* put a verb in your headline. Not only does it help your reader (by creating more action right up front), but it also helps you arrive at a more effective opening sentence.

Want proof of how universal this technique is in publishing? Leaf through today's newspaper. You'll be hard-pressed to find a headline without a verb in it. (Sometimes the verb is implied. For example, when you read *Three Keys to Better Health*, your mind inserts a word like *Getting* or *Acquiring* before *Better*.)

Right now you may be saying to yourself, "Well, if the headline has a verb in it, couldn't you use it as a lead sentence?" The answer is yes. Although professional writers seldom write their own headlines (this is usually an editor's job), they often *pretend* they're doing so if they're having trouble composing a good lead sentence.

Try it with your students. Give them a writing assignment on any topic. Tell them to write nothing but the headline. It has to have a verb, and it has to be short enough to *look* like a headline. (Seven or eight words, tops.) To make it a little easier, remind them of another headline-writing rule in the publishing business: Avoid starting with an article (words like *a* and *the*). Here are some examples they can keep in mind:

- Man Bites Dog
- Why Johnny Can't Read
- War Is Over

## How To Get a "Yes"

Professional writers use a simple, time-tested trick to get people to say yes when they're asking for help: they give their reader a chance to say no to part of the request without saying no to the whole thing. How? By asking for *time* as well as *help*. In other words, if you want someone to help you or loan you money or do anything else they might not want to do, frame the request as a plea for some of their time. This lets people say no to the time instead of to your real request.

For example, what's the worst thing I could say to you if you asked me: *Will you have twenty minutes sometime this morning to help me sort through the old clothes in my closet?*

Even if I gave you an outright *no*, you could easily follow up with: *Well, when's a more convenient time?* Maybe I can't spare twenty minutes for you this morning. But I know I can give you twenty minutes sometime soon. So, my likely response is going to be: *No, not this morning. But we can do it later this afternoon, if that's OK.*

As the kids get better at this, they'll learn to lay out some more specific options as they make their requests: *Will you have twenty minutes sometime this morning to help me sort through the old clothes in my closet? If this morning isn't convenient, we could do it this afternoon.*

Some requests are more urgent. In those cases, convey the urgency with facts: *Will you have twenty minutes sometime this morning to help me sort through the old clothes in my closet? I'd love to postpone it to this afternoon, but Dad wants me to help him clean out the garage then.*

Teaching this trick is fun. Your students will use it in real life nearly every day. It adds to their understanding of writing as precise communication. Get them talking about things they have to request from parents or siblings. Money will come up, of course. So will rides to friends' houses. Sisters often ask to borrow each other's clothes. Older kids ask younger siblings for help with chores. List these on the board and explore ways to frame the request in *time* form:

- *Dad, can we sit down for a few minutes tonight and talk about money for my class trip?*

- *Mom, Terry asked me to come over this afternoon. When do you think you'll have fifteen minutes to drive me over there?*

- *Sis, is next Tuesday a good day for me to borrow that cool top for school?*

- *Hey, Tommy, do you have ten minutes to help me rake leaves before your friends come over?*

Despite how simple and effective this technique is, people rarely use it. In fact, people generally don't "ask" for help, at all. They demand it, by putting their request in the form of a declarative statement such as, *I need help cleaning out my closet.* It's too easy to say no to a request like that.

Want to demonstrate this to the class? Have them go back to your list of household requests and write two different versions of each request: a declarative one (*I need . . .* or *I want . . .*) and a gentle one that includes alternatives and details. For example, say the school is selling souvenir sweatshirts and other apparel. The declarative version of a request might say:

> *Mom and Dad, I need $25 for a school sweatshirt.*

The gentler one asks:

> *Mom and Dad, may I please buy a school sweatshirt? They're $25, but if that's too much maybe I can just buy a school cap or scarf. Or, maybe I can wait until next week.*

Do this with a couple of requests and they'll get the idea pretty quickly. Oh, and remind them to say "please."

## Give your reader some credit!

Good writers also give their readers credit for some intelligence. That means they don't waste words on something their reader already knows. The first example that comes to mind is the universal opening for sales letters: *Enclosed is . . .* Every time I read that line I want to ask: "What kind of moron do you think I am? You don't have to tell me what's enclosed! I can see you've sent me something. Don't insult my intelligence by telling me what I already know. Tell me what you want me to do with the stuff."

Kids break this rule often—without even knowing it. They'll start off a term paper about World War II with a sentence like: *World War II changed Europe in many ways.* Or they'll lead off an essay about education by telling you: *Education is the key to a better life.* I call these "non-leads." They say nothing, essentially. They're just empty words taking up space but performing no useful purpose.

An easy way to discourage this habit—and to encourage kids to write reader-challenging leads—is an assignment I call "Tell me something cool." Make a list of ten or fifteen subjects and ask the kids to "tell you something cool" about each one.

The trick is to make the subjects very common, so the kids have to really research them to find something you wouldn't already know about them. Here are some examples:

- Your school
- Cats
- Soccer
- Electricity
- The dollar bill

If they search hard enough, they should be able to find some fascinating facts about any of these. The value of this assignment is it teaches kids that no subject has to be boring. It's their responsibility as writers to make it interesting and challenging to their reader. When they get the idea, you can move on to a more elaborate version of this assignment, called "Make 'em say 'Wow!' which I describe in the next chapter.

 ## How the Pros Write Letters

How do you write a letter complaining about bad service? How do you write to someone you're angry at? How do you answer a Help Wanted ad? What's the most carefully and frequently read part of a letter? Before we talk about how to teach these skills, let me answer those questions:

1. Make it an act of friendship.
2. Pretend the person you're mad at is either the world heavyweight boxing champ or a member of the clergy.
3. Ask for an interview, not a job.
4. The *P.S.*

Let's go back and take these one by one.

Writing an effective complaint letter is a valuable life skill that's best learned early. All of us occasionally have to tell a neighbor or business establishment in writing that they've committed some sort of wrong against us.

Turn the complaint into an act of courtesy or friendship. Always start the letter by acknowledging your role in the dispute.

- *Please tell me if you think I'm overreacting. But lately, I've noticed you're letting your dog . . .*

- *You might be angry after reading this, and I don't blame you. But I have to tell you about something that's been bothering me. Lately, I've noticed you're letting your dog . . .*

- *Will you consider a small request from a neighbor? Lately, I've noticed you're letting your dog . . .*

Of course, it's not easy convincing yourself to temper your perfectly justified anger into the kind of humility that inspires a friendly response. A trick I use is to imagine I'm addressing a person of great authority or stature. For example, I try to imagine how the heavyweight champ might react if he were the target of my letter—and if he were sitting next to me while reading it. How much tough-talking would I do? Name-calling? Posturing? Not much. I'd tiptoe in like a little churchmouse.

Try this with your class. Ask them to list three major complaints in their lives and to write two letters to whomever is causing them. One is an angry letter (the one they'd like to write). The other is designed to get results (it would be respectful and understanding as though it were directed at someone you wouldn't dare anger, such as a member of the clergy . . . or the heavyweight boxing champ). Have some students read their *before* and *after* letters aloud in class, if you want. Kids love imagining a boxing champ's reaction to the angry versions.

How to answer a Want Ad is another key letter-writing skill kids need to learn. A fun way to teach this is to have some parents contribute Want Ads for jobs around their homes (babysitter, lawn care, car wash, hedge trimmer, phone message-taker . . . whatever chores they can come up with). Let the kids write letters applying for the job of their choice, but with fictitious names. And have the parents evaluate them for effectiveness. If this runs true to form, the chosen letters will exhibit many of the following traits:

- **A name in the salutation.** It will say *Dear Mr. Jones* instead of *Dear Sir.* It won't say, *To whom it may concern.* If the ad doesn't give a name, then the writer shouldn't use a salutation. They should just start with the text of the letter itself.

- **A two-sentence opening paragraph.** The first sentence asks for an interview: *Please consider interviewing me for the babysitting job you advertised in yesterday's newspaper.* The second summarizes why you should get the interview: *I'm sixteen years old and have babysat for nine different families with kids ranging in age from two to thirteen.*

- **A paragraph telling why you like doing what this job requires.** Two or three sentences is plenty. *I enjoy playing games with young children. And I like the look on parents' faces when they come home to a quiet, tidy house.*

- **A paragraph highlighting some of your other fine qualities.** Again, keep it brief. *I'm a member of Student Government and the Track team. And I'm secretary of the Key Club.*

- **A one-sentence close that again asks for an interview.** *I'm anxious to learn more about the job and I hope you'll call me to talk soon.*

The letter should contain one last element—the one that their reader will probably read first and then reread after he's gone through the rest of the text: a *P.S.* summarizing one of your main points.

> *P.S. Not many kids my age have babysat for so many different clients. I hope you agree that's a good reason for us to meet.*

The *P.S.* is the most often read part of any letter. That's exactly why ad writers put them into the junk-mail letters you see every day. People can't help but scan to the bottom of the letter and read what's at the very end. Encourage your students to use this little trick.

## ▚ Tricks Writers *Don't* Use

A common mistake among inexperienced writers is thinking they have to write a title or headline before starting the actual assignment. This is usually an invitation to frustration. Insist that your students focus on conveying the information, not coming up with a fancy title for their composition. In fact, if you really want to ease their mind about this, tell them not to put a headline on the piece at all.

Professional writers rarely try to write a title or headline for an article before they start writing. (Actually, as I mentioned earlier, authors don't usually write headlines, anyway. Editors do.) The exception is when they're struggling to find a good opening sentence. In that case, they'll often play with some headline options to help them focus on an article's main or most compelling points.

## ▚ When To Be *Un*-Creative

Finally and perhaps most importantly, professional writers know when to be simple and effective instead of clever and creative. See if this sounds familiar. You're writing a letter to a friend about an incident that made you really happy. And you want to convey just how happy you were. So you write:

> *I was as happy as a . . .*
> *as a . . .*
> *. . . er . . . as a . . .*

And the word doesn't come. No matter how hard you try, you can't think of a clever description of just how happy you are. So you give up and use something risk-free (read: boring), like, *as happy as a lark*.

Why not just say *I was really happy?* Or, *I haven't been that happy in a long time?* Or, *I can't even remember when I've been that happy?* I know they're not clever. But at least they're clear and honest.

Students go through this every time their teacher tells them to "be creative . . . don't settle for common, everyday language . . . add some descriptive flair to your writing." They struggle and wince and grow more frustrated by the minute. They complain of having writer's block. And it's all unnecessary. You can't force creativity and there's no need to. Simple sentences are just as effective as creative ones when the goal is to convey a common, everyday message.

The best way I know to teach this is with published examples. Have students scour newspapers and magazines for sentences containing similes and metaphors. Write them on the board or turn them into a worksheet. Then have the kids rewrite them in un-clever ways. *Meaner than a junkyard dog* becomes simply *very mean*. *Whining like a slow-leaking tire* becomes *squealing*. And so on.

Seasoned, professional writers do this all the time. When they can't come up with a clever way to say something, they default to clear and simple. But they don't cop out and go for the cheap cliché. Like I said, they're not always real creative. Just effective.

# Chapter 5

# Ten Lessons to Get You Started

## Here's How to Make a Big Impact on Kids' Writing Immediately

This may be the first chapter you read. If it is, I'm not surprised. Most teachers I know want to change things, not just read about them. And the best way to change kids' writing habits is to start breaking the old ones and teaching the new ones right away. These ten lessons will help you do just that. They deal with five habits that I think can make the quickest positive impact on students' writing:

- Defining the audience and purpose
- Getting the reader interested
- Economizing words
- Backing up opinions
- Recognizing and purging common bad writing habits

There's a logical order to these. Defining the audience and purpose is the most fundamental of all good writing habits. That's why it's the subject of the first three lessons.

Next comes writing strong opening sentences to capture your reader's interest right away. I've listed two lessons on that subject. One gives students a way to write compelling and unpredictable lead sentences. The other helps them zero in on their main point before they start writing. Then come two lessons on keeping words and sentences simple and easy to read. The final two lessons are aimed at teaching kids to edit their own bad habits out of their writing.

## ◎ 1. People and Purpose, Part I

Clip out articles from a variety of magazines. Preview them so you and the kids will be able to identify the audience and purpose the writer had in mind. Then photocopy them, pass them out and talk with the class about the audience and purpose they think the writer was targeting. See how close they can come to identifying the kind of magazine it came from.

Try to find magazines representing various audiences: kids, women, men, homeowners, gardeners, car enthusiasts. If you subscribe to any niche-targeted magazines—say, about computers or needlepoint or antiques—they'll make great sources. Look for articles that have one or more of the following purposes:

- **Request** (These are rare in magazines; you might find an article or two asking you to respond to a survey, though.)
- **Inform** (News magazines are a good source.)
- **Teach** (Recipes do this; so does most any article in a how-to magazine.)
- **Entertain** (Examples include funny or poignant stories, and humor columns.)

Do this exercise a few times and you'll have laid the groundwork for . . .

## ◎ 2. People and Purpose, Part II

You did the work last time. Now it's the kids' turn. Have them write four different paragraphs about the same subject and for the same audience, but each designed with a different purpose: *request, inform, teach,* and *entertain.* Select some to be read aloud, and let the other students try to identify the purpose.

The topics should lend themselves fairly easily to the different purposes. For example, skiing. In the *request* version, the student could be asking for money for skis. The *inform* version could be a list of skiing's greatest risks and benefits. The *teach* version could be about (what else?) how to ski. And the *entertain* piece could be either serious (for example, *conquering the mountain for the first time*) or humorous (*conquering the ski lodge for the first time*). You could follow the same pattern for car buying, gardening, sewing a button onto a shirt, making a cake, and so on.

That's the *purpose* version of this assignment. There's an *audience* version too. Have the students write four versions of a paragraph, all with the same purpose but each aimed at a different audience. I'd suggest these:

- Senior citizen
- Woman
- Man
- Teacher

For example, have them write a paragraph designed to sell the desk chair they're sitting on to each of those four people. Or a paragraph designed to teach each of those people how to surf the Internet. Pick things that are of real interest to each audience. Don't pick simple items like a pencil; that'll force the kids to make up benefits that don't exist.

And discuss the things each person would value most about the item you're trying to sell them. A senior citizen might value a chair's low center of gravity (so it's easier to get in and out of). A woman might value its light weight (so she can move it around easily). And so on.

### ◉ 3. "Hey Mr. Rolex, wanna buy a watch?"

Poorly focused writing occurs when a student can't or won't take time to visualize his target audience. Here's a fun way to show kids how important it is to picture their reader before they write. You'll need an assistant to help you with this one. A friend or another teacher will do fine.

Ask the students to imagine they own a store (let each student decide individually what kind of store). They're so badly in need of a customer that they're ready to offer a huge discount on a big piece of merchandise (again, students' choice) to the first person they see.

Well, it so happens that person is your helper, who's standing in front of the class in full disguise, so the students can't determine his or her gender or age. (If you want a more elaborate ruse, have your friend pose outside a window visible from your classroom. Make sure he or she is either in disguise or is far enough away to be indistinguishable as man, woman, young or old.)

"See that stranger?" you'll say to the class. "I want you to write this person a letter offering a huge discount on a piece of merchandise in your store. Do everything you can to make the item sound as appealing as possible to the person. Feel free to include any other incentives you can think of to get this person into your store."

Obviously, the students will have to guess at how to make their offer appealing. Some will guess right. Others will be way off. One or two sharp students might just raise their hand and start asking questions about the stranger. If they do, congratulate them for having the good sense not to start writing without knowing who their reader is. (Whether you answer the questions or just make them play along is up to you. I'd probably make them play along.)

After the kids have written their letters, unmask your helper and have some students read their sales letters out loud. Everyone should get a lot of laughs over how poorly targeted some of them are. Of course, when you're all through laughing, you'll ask the students to rewrite their letters with a focus toward their actual—and now visible—reader.

## ◎ 4. Make 'em say "Wow!"

Good writing starts with a good lead sentence. I can't overemphasize this. When you help students learn the skill of lead-sentence writing, you help them overcome the dreaded *how-do-I-start?* syndrome. And that almost guarantees a better overall piece of writing.

The secret to writing compelling lead sentences is in thinking compelling thoughts. And believe it or not, you *can* train kids to do that. The first step is making them find several unique facts about some simple topics. Earlier I described a lesson called "Tell me something cool" for doing just this (see Chapter 4).

The next step is making them apply this skill with more complex topics. Or, as I like to say, "Start your report with a sentence that'll make me say 'Wow!'"

Think about it. How would your students typically lead off a report on *windmills* or on *the life and times of William Henry Harrison*? You can almost predict it, can't you?

- *Windmills convert wind energy into power for grinding grain, pumping water, or generating electricity.*

- *William Henry Harrison, the ninth president of the United States, was born on February 9, 1773, in Charles County, VA.*

Kids have no more fun writing those sentences—or the reports that follow them—than you have reading them. The way to change that is to make them find and lead off with a unique or fascinating fact about the topic.

To introduce the idea, give your students ten or twenty report topics and ask them to find just one *wow* fact about each. Tell them to write the fact down but not to worry about turning it into a compelling sentence. You'll do that together in class.

Take the subject of windmills, for example. Most any encyclopedia article on windmills has to explain that wind is the result of circulating air, alternately cooling and being heated by the sun. The average person doesn't know that. Does that fact give you any ideas for a lead sentence? How about this one: *Windmills were the earth's first solar energy source.*

Or take William Henry Harrison. He retired from politics in 1829. He did return to run for president in 1836 but lost to Martin Van Buren. So it wasn't until his inauguration in March 1841 at age 68—after 12 years of retirement—that he actually resumed his political career. A month later, he died of pneumonia, caused (some say) by the stress of taking on such a demanding job after many years of relaxation. Toss these facts around in class and sooner or later you and the students should come upon a pretty neat lead: *His official cause of death was pneumonia. But many people believe it was the presidency itself that killed William Henry Harrison.*

I'm not going to pretend this process will come naturally to you or your class. It takes practice. But it's not impossible and the reward is well worth the effort. Just stay with it. Your writing assignments have to start off as research and thinking assignments. Make the kids find some little-known facts, and then help them massage those facts into sentences that provoke "wows." This is *teaching* writing. It's about discovery and discussion.

Expect lots of awkward-sounding lead sentences at first. That's fine. They're learning a new skill, a new and better habit. Their first attempts are bound to be weak. But failure is not an option. You have to persist until they get it, the same way you would with key skills in any other subject.

### ◎ 5. "You have twenty seconds to sell me."

Not all writing assignments lend themselves well to *wow* facts in their lead sentences. For example, if you asked students to compare and contrast the beliefs of two government leaders, you wouldn't expect them to start off with a fascinating fact about them. (A clever student could probably come up with one, but it would likely get in the way.) Nor would you expect a *wow* fact in the opening sentence of a personal letter, a summary of a science experiment or an opinion piece.

But no matter what you're writing, it's always important to start strong. That's because in most types of writing you have about twenty seconds to get your readers' attention. If you don't get them within that time, they're gone.

I mentioned earlier in the book that TV episode summaries are great examples of quick-reading, info-packed opening sentences. Use them as your classroom model for snappy sentence writing that makes your point without testing your reader's patience. Have students practice summarizing their favorite books or TV episodes in one sentence. Tell them to summarize at least one show a day for a month.

In reading or literature classes, have them do one-sentence story summaries like miniature book reports. In history or social studies, give them quizzes with five or ten essay questions requiring single-sentence answers.

Pick a few writing samples each day and read them aloud in class. Leave out the authors' names, if you like—although, the kids will almost always give themselves away by slouching down in their chairs, grinning sheepishly, and glancing around the room. Ask the students what makes each sentence good or bad. Good ones leave you with some vital or striking pieces of information as well as a desire to ask questions and keep reading. Bad ones sound like old news or no news.

Remember, you're doing more than just teaching a writing skill here. You're creating awareness of good and bad writing, and you're removing the ego from writing criticism. (Why is it we're fine when someone points out a math error we've committed, but we take great offense when people critique our writing?)

Snappy sentence writing is one of those skills that pays great dividends as kids grow older and get jobs. The average manager reads a hundred or more written documents every day. E-mail, interoffice memos, project proposals, sticky notes, job-application letters . . . you name it. Employees and job applicants who can't quickly summarize their main point get lost and forgotten. Let's teach students to write with respect for the average person's precious, limited amount of reading time.

## ◎ 6. Find the Wasted Words

Excess verbiage is probably the most common bad habit among writers of any age. You should make word economy a key goal of your writing instruction as early as possible.

An easy way to introduce the idea is simply to make up phrases and sentences with unnecessary words in them. Have the kids identify the "wasted" words, discuss why they're unnecessary for effective writing, and then rewrite the sentences without them. Start with obvious examples like these (the unnecessary words are in italics):

- *Sharp, pointy* fangs (All fangs are assumed to be sharp and pointy. That's why we call them fangs! You only need a modifier for the fangs if you're talking about *dull* or *broken* ones. Or *bloody* ones.)

- Big, red, *air-filled* balloon (Again, when you're talking about a balloon, you expect it to be filled with air. A *burst* or *deflated* balloon needs description because it's a departure from the norm. On the other hand, not all balloons are *big* or *red*, so you can't omit those words without losing meaning.)

- *Freezing*, cold water (If the water is truly frozen, then omit *cold*, because all freezing water is cold. But if it's just very cold, don't say it's *freezing* if it's only frigid. *Freezing* means *ice* to most people.)
- *Big*, tall building (Again, if you tell me the building is *tall*, you don't need to tell me it's *big*, too. *Tall* has already told me that.)

You can have the students make up and correct their own examples, too.

Once the kids can spot the obviously wasted words, move onto more subtle ones like these:

- *Loud, scary* explosion (The typical explosion is *loud* and *scary*. If the volume is important to the story, then use more specific terms. For example, tell me how far away the blast could be heard or how many windows it shattered: *Suddenly there came an explosion that toppled the juice glasses right out of our kitchen cabinet.* Other reasons to modify the explosion would be if it were *muffled* or *distant*—anything that made it out-of-the-ordinary. But if the volume isn't critical to your point, don't modify *explosion* unnecessarily. It just adds words.)
- *Rear* taillights or *front* headlights (They seem obvious but they show up a lot in careless writing.)
- *Huge* giant (See, you've caught on already.)

Finally, here are some examples with wasted words that are a little trickier to spot:

- *High* in the sky (*In the sky* is all you need. If something's really high, use more precise language such as *in the clouds* or *in the stratosphere.*)
- Made a *new* discovery (*Discovery* already tells me it was something new.)

Spend lots of time on this and be sure to start with the easy examples first. And, again, after the kids show they can replace wasted words in your phrases and sentences, let them do the same with phrases and sentences they make up themselves. That will introduce the process of self-editing.

Remember, the goal is to make kids aware of how easily wasted words can creep into their writing. Wasted words aren't wrong. They're just unnecessary. They slow reading and can muddle the meaning of your sentences. They're like wearing two pairs of gloves. Instead of adding warmth, they chill your hands by constricting circulation and creating sweat.

## ◎ 7. Comma Cacophony

Comma abuse takes two forms: misuse and overuse. People misuse commas when they treat them like periods. Here are two examples from E-mails I recently read. Both of them clearly contain two separate sentences.

- *I called the guy for the second time, he wasn't in the first time I called.*
- *Please let me know whether you'll attend, I have to confirm attendance with the hotel.*

This is more than just a bad writing habit. It's also grammatically incorrect. The remedy is making students write their own double-sentence sentences and then rewrite them without the comma. You can make up the incorrect sentences yourself, if you like. But I think kids get more out of the lesson if they have to write the before and after versions themselves.

Comma overuse is just as easy to spot but it's a little tougher to correct. Whether or not a sentence contains too many commas can be very subjective. Instead of right or wrong, you should present this as a *better-or-worse* concept. A sentence containing five commas may be grammatically correct. But breaking it up into a few sentences is almost always better.

For practice, try something I call "comma cacophany." Have the students write twenty-five sentences, each containing at least three commas. Then have them rewrite each sentence with no more than one comma apiece. (Yes, it's OK to break each one up into two or three sentences.)

Let the class have fun with their original comma-heavy sentences. The longer and more complicated and choppy-sounding, the better. It's actually pretty hard to write a sentence with three commas. Try it yourself, and you'll see why this is such an effective teaching tool. The kids will quickly learn to recognize the need to economize on sentence length and avoid unnecessary clauses and phrases.

# ⊙ 8. "Here are five reasons why..."

Kids love giving their opinions about things. If you're ever struggling to motivate your class to just write something . . . *anything* . . . give them an *opinion* assignment. The subject doesn't matter. It can be simple, such as "My favorite food" or "What kind of day did I have today?" Or it can be complex, such as "Why democracy is the world's best government system" or "History's most important inventor."

But there's a key to writing opinions effectively: You have to support them with facts. Notice I didn't say you have to prove them. You just have to *support* them, which means giving reasons why you believe what you believe. It's another one of those obligations that writers have to fulfill. (Professional writers have a saying about people who spout uninformed and unsupported opinions: "He doesn't like it when the facts get in the way of his opinion.")

Citing facts doesn't make your opinion right. It just validates your belief. Your opinion is actually your interpretation of the facts.

Teach opinion-writing as a two-step process. Step One is gathering and listing the facts—just the facts. Step Two is lining them up in *pro* and *con* columns and then writing about them. Say you've assigned an opinion essay on "My favorite food." Whatever food your students pick—let's say it's lettuce—they have to list some facts about it. Those might include everything from its nutritional profile and its value in different recipes, to how it's grown, what it costs, and how it tastes.

Make the kids list these facts in two columns: those that support their opinion and those that refute it. They may need a third column for facts that are neutral. For example, the fact that lettuce is green shouldn't affect its choice as a student's favorite food—unless, of course, the student's favorite color is green.

Once they've done all that, they can start writing. Encourage the kids to lead off their first attempts at opinion-writing with a sentence like this: *My favorite food is lettuce and here are five reasons why.* They should then list all the reasons and do their best to elaborate on those they think are the most powerful. They also should list the negatives and elaborate on the strongest of those.

I recommend starting with very simple topics when you set out to teach this concept:

- *Today was a great day.*
- *Summer is the best season for sports.*
- *Milk is nature's most perfect food.*

Give several assignments like those before you go on to trickier ones such as:

- *Earthquakes are nature's most awesome force.*
- *John F. Kennedy was America's greatest president.*
- *The automobile changed America more than any other invention.*

Be careful not to discourage students from writing what they think. The point of this lesson is to teach them how to support their opinion, not to avoid having one.

## ◎ 9. Writing the World's Worst Essay

Here's a fun way to help kids recognize and fix bad writing habits: Let them write an *intentionally lousy* first draft of a composition. Tell them you want them to get all their bad writing habits out of their system.

I've done a version of this with salespeople: I've asked them to write me "the world's worst sales letter." They have great fun packing it full of overused expressions, convoluted language, and gratuitous compliments. When they're through, they look at what they've written and vow never to send a letter to a customer or prospect without first checking it for bad writing habits.

Here's how the technique works with kids: Assign them a composition on their choice of, say, three different subjects. Vary the topics (as well as the intended audience and purpose) so everyone in the class can find something fun to write about.

Tell the students: "Your goal is to demonstrate as many bad writing habits as you can, and to ignore as many good ones as you can. Write a long, boring lead sentence full of stuff that your target reader won't understand or care about. Use the passive voice as much as possible. Pack it with big words and long sentences full of commas, so it sounds like you're trying to impress your reader instead of communicate with him. Toss around lots of opinions with no facts to back them up. In other words, totally ignore your audience and purpose."

Here are some suggested topics. Feel free to try them out or make up some of your own.

- Instructions for a student who just moved to your school, telling him how to become popular among the other kids

- A letter to the school principal, convincing her that schools should never abolish summer vacation

- An essay for your parents, comparing your favorite music star to theirs

- A report about the United States President, designed to explain to a foreigner why you would or wouldn't vote for him

- A plan for getting the kind of job you'll want as an adult, to be read by your teacher (that's you)

- A letter to your next-door neighbor whose loud stereo is keeping you awake at night

- A brochure designed to sell your favorite video game to a grandparent or other adult relative besides your parents

- A report teaching a first grader how rubber is made

If you're thinking these might make good topics for serious writing assignments, you're right. That's exactly what you'll do with them next. But read on.

When the kids are through, pick a few really bad samples on each topic and have the authors read them aloud. You may need to reassure everyone that this was for fun and that you know they purposely wrote these poorly. Ask the class to jot down all the bad writing habits they hear in the samples. You should do the same. List these on the board after each reading. After awhile, you'll hear some common themes in the students' critiques:

"Boring."

"Confusing."

"Doesn't make any sense."

"Wrong."

"Insulting."

Make sure you draw the kids out on these. "Why is this boring? Is it the topic or just the way they wrote about it? If it's the writing, what's the problem? Too many big words? Stiff language that doesn't sound like a real person speaking?" Remember, this is an awareness exercise. As with most lessons in this book, the discussion is as important as the writing itself. If you and the kids don't have some real laughs in between the learning, you probably made the assignment sound too serious.

After you've had a good classroom critique of the *before* versions, have the kids rewrite them—this time with proper focus on their audience and purpose.

You might want to have students write intentionally bad first drafts of the next few serious writing projects you assign. Or at least give them the option of doing it. It's a great way to foster self-editing skills without the pressure of trying to compose a serious draft right out of the chute.

## ◎ 10. Editing the World's Worst Writing

Editing someone else's poor writing is one of the most effective and eye-opening activities you can assign your students. That's especially true if you tell them what kinds of bad writing habits to look for—and if the poor writing comes from a published source.

Believe it or not, you can find plenty of poor writing examples in published works. Some of the worst are in textbooks (especially at the high school level), scientific journals (finding bad writing by academics is like shooting fish in a barrel) and so-called "classic" novels. I believe the often plodding, pompous language kids read in these works is a major turnoff. We need to acknowledge this instead of pretending it's the kids who are at fault.

Now, you're probably saying to yourself: "Just because it makes the kids think, that doesn't mean it's bad writing. Besides, who is he to criticize classic literature?" I'm not criticizing classic literature, and I'm certainly not recommending we eliminate these chestnuts from our curricula. I'm only saying we shouldn't hold them up as examples of clear, effective written communication for kids to emulate. It's the stories that are classics, not the writing mechanics. (Otherwise, we'd be teaching kids to write essays in iambic pentameter, just like Shakespeare used for his plays.)

Besides, when you read a novel you do it voluntarily—and usually as a form of relaxation. You expect to concentrate on it amid all kinds of distractions. And you don't mind having to reread passages a few times to get the point. That's not the case with the things people read on their jobs and in their everyday lives. We want brevity and clarity, and we want it now. We don't have time to search for the main point. If you make me work too hard to find your message, I'll get frustrated. Our main goal is to teach writing skills that improve communication. Novel- and story-writing have no place in this process.

Here's a three-step mini-curriculum to help kids learn to turn unclear, ineffective writing into clear, effective writing.

## Step 1: Edit Words

Start by asking the class to list on the board all the boring-sounding words they can think of, without opening a dictionary.

Try not to get hung up defining *boring*. There are no right or wrong answers in this exercise. Write down any words the kids suggest. Then go back over them and have the class suggest simpler-sounding alternatives.

The *boring* and *better* words will vary by grade level, of course. You can jump-start the lesson for elementary-school students by giving examples like *merely, cannot,* and *gratitude.* (The improved versions of these words will depend on context, but three examples are *just, can't,* and *thanks.*) Older kids will catch on if you use examples like *ideology, utilize,* and *induce.* (Improved versions: *belief, use,* and *cause.*)

Allow the students to replace the pompous words with either a single word or a phrase, as long as the replacement is simpler and clearer. Clarity and simplicity are more important than word economy in this particular case. For example, they might replace *incarcerated* with *jailed, locked up,* or *put behind bars.*

This lesson serves much the same purpose as those lists of good and bad words you find in most writing texts. But it's better, because it forces the kids to make up their own lists. It's the exercise of doing that—not just reading and memorizing the good and bad words—that teaches students how to spot and fix bad writing.

Once you've done a few sessions like this, turn the kids loose to find and edit some pomposities in published works: "For homework, I want you to find twenty unnecessarily big words in published sources. Write them down and tell me what smaller word or words you'd use instead of the big ones. If you have to look up the big word in a dictionary to help you find a replacement, good. That'll help you understand what your readers go through when you try to impress them with big words."

Don't tell the kids where to look for the big words. But do ask them to list the published works they used to find them. It'll give you some clues about where kids expect to find boring writing.

## Step 2: Edit Sentences

It's easy to expand the word-editing lesson into one for full sentences. You may want to start right out using published examples though. It gets tedious trying to make up lists of long, pompous-sounding sentences yourself and then rewriting them, too.

Let the kids hunt for examples of ponderously long sentences on their own. Tell them to look for sentences containing at least forty words. They'll bring in some doozies. (You might even offer a prize to the student who finds the longest published sentence—a giant eraser or a little pillow where they can rest their word-weary head.) After some class discussion, they'll surprise you with their ability to rewrite the sentences in clearer, more effective language. Again, be sure to tell them they always have the option of turning one sentence into two or three.

## Step 3: Edit Paragraphs

I recommend you find a few published examples of long, boring paragraphs for the students to edit. That way you'll avoid the risk of making the kids rewrite something out of context. Look for paragraphs that seem to drone on forever. Anything more than ten sentences is a good candidate. You'll know you have a winner if most of the sentences are very long and contain a hefty dose of obvious five-dollar words.

As the kids edit these paragraphs, focus mainly on how they rewrite the individual words and sentences. Look for how well they shorten big words into smaller words or simpler phrases, and how well they break up droning sentences into two or three tighter ones.

# Conclusion
## The Secret Ingredient in Good Writing

"I'll be brief." That's probably the most powerful opening line a public speaker can use. It helps us audience members focus immediately on the speaker's message instead of on our discomfort and our watches. We can only guess whether "brief" means ten minutes or an hour. But it doesn't matter. The speech always seems shorter if we believe the speaker plans to get right to the point.

Why do seasoned speakers use that opening line so often? What motivates them to offer us such reassurance right up front? In a word: courtesy. They know that our attentiveness is a privilege. And they don't want to abuse that privilege by launching into a rambling, self-indulgent discourse. They know their job is to give us what we've come for, and then to leave the podium.

Courtesy is the key ingredient in good writing, too. It's really what this book is all about. Courtesy is why kids should give their readers as much key information as possible in their lead sentence. It's why the word *you* is such an effective opener to personal correspondence. It's why small words are better than big ones, and why short, snappy sentences are better than long, rambling ones. Courtesy is why we should use active verbs and keep anger out of our writing. In short, "Be courteous to your reader" is the first writing rule that we should teach kids.

As they write, students should picture their audience fidgeting in their seats, glancing at the clock and wondering when they can leave. They should assume that more than half of their readers want to leave after the first three sentences. Tell them the important stuff before you lose them.

Assume a small group of readers will stick around for another few paragraphs. And assume that only a hardy handful will continue reading to the bitter end. Honor these diehards by continuing to write in the same clear, simple language you used in the very first sentence.

It's the courteous thing to do.

Let me know if you agree.

Mike Brusko, 6563 Sweetbriar Lane, Zionsville, PA 18092. E-mail: Writewell9@aol.com

# *Recommended Reading*

Don't look for a list of how-to-write books on this page. The books that have most influenced my thinking on the subject come in three flavors:

- Those dealing with semantics and effective communication strategies
- Those that try to simplify complex subjects
- Those that challenge conventional wisdom

I read them to recharge and refresh, to refine and refocus. If I've convinced you that writing is first and foremost a life skill, and that we can all do it effectively with a little practice and the right fundamentals, you'll enjoy these books a lot.

Carville, James. 1996. *We're Right, They're Wrong*. New York: Random House.

Davis, Kenneth C. 1990. *Don't Know Much About History*. New York: Avon Books.

———. 1998. *Don't Know Much About the Bible*. New York: Eaglebrook/Morrow.

Dershowitz, Alan. 1992. *Contrary to Popular Opinion*. New York: Berkley Books.

Elgin, Suzette Haden. 1980. *The Gentle Art of Verbal Self-Defense*. Paramus, NJ: Prentice-Hall Inc.

Franken, Al. 1996. *Rush Limbaugh Is a Big Fat Idiot (and Other Observations)*. New York: Delacorte Press.

Harmon, Ronald. 1994. *Caution! English.* Boston, MA: Heinle & Heinle.

Macaulay, David. 1988. *The Way Things Work.* Boston, MA: Houghton Mifflin Co.

O'Rourke, P. J. 1994. *All the Trouble in the World.* New York: Atlantic Monthly Press.

Spence, Gerry. 1995. *How to Argue and Win Every Time.* New York: St. Martin's Press.

Spong, John Shelby. 1992. *Rescuing the Bible from Fundamentalism.* San Francisco: Harper San Francisco.